Advance Praise for *BrandingPays*™

"Karen is <u>the</u> master of personal branding."
Regis McKenna, Silicon Valley marketing guru and author

"This book is a goldmine! It will transform how you brand yourself and your company. The BrandingPays system works."
Cristina Nogueira, Partner, Walking the Talk,
and former Sales & Marketing Director at Microsoft

"Karen had a methodology for personal branding before anyone knew what it was. This book is destined to be a classic."
Susan Lucas-Conwell, former CEO, Great Place to Work

"Karen helped my company to create a powerful brand position from scratch and transform the way we approach and attract customers in today's global market. Her book will do the same for my own personal brand."
Ryan (Young K.) Yoo, Vice President,
Global Sales and Marketing, Park Systems

"This is a must-read if you're ready to invest in YOU! Create your personal brand by design versus by default. I experienced a mind-set shift in how I saw myself and my potential."
Monica L. Poindexter, Head of Diversity and Inclusion, Genentech

"This book is a no-nonsense, practical, operational, data-based and strategically sound method for improving everyone's personal brand. It also is very easy to read and understand. Kudos!"
Leonard Lodish, Samuel R. Harrell Professor of Marketing,
Wharton School, University of Pennsylvania

"The wait is over! Karen's expert advice that has catapulted me and my organizations to better outcomes for years is now available 'on demand.' This book is one you'll want to own and revisit again and again."
Maureen E. McNulty, Senior Director of Development, Principal and Major Gifts, Harvard Medical School

"BrandingPays is fabulous! It's a practical book chock full of examples and templates that will help anyone be their best brand. Karen Kang is the master of strategic personal branding."
Rene Shimada Siegal, President and founder, High Tech Connect,
and regular contributor to Inc.com

"BrandingPays is a must-read for entrepreneurs and professionals looking to differentiate themselves in competitive and crowded markets. Strategic personal branding is something anyone can achieve and the book's practical approach includes examples that make total sense."

Jack Koch, Managing Partner, ProRelevant
and former 3Com Vice President of Marketing

"BrandingPays is a compelling and actionable book that readers will find highly useful. It should be a reference on every professional's bookshelf. I utilize Karen's personal branding lessons all of the time both at work and in my personal life with excellent results."

Caryn McDowell, Executive Director, Corporate Law, Affymax, Inc.

"I first met Karen when I had just embarked on my entrepreneurial journey. In the course of two days, she transformed the way I positioned myself, my business idea and the path forward. She has a remarkable ability to extract the essence of a person's brand equity. This book is a great distillation of all of her years of experience. I would highly recommend it for executives and entrepreneurs alike."

Satya Krishnaswamy, CEO, NextPrinciples,
and former Global Vice President, Office of the CTO, SAP Labs

"A must-have for all professionals looking to up-level their impact. The easy-to-use BrandingPays System helped me clarify and communicate powerfully the value I deliver to my clients."

Marc Levine, Ph.D., Executive and Team Coach, Marc Levine & Co.

"BrandingPays delivers aha! moments from start to finish. If you want to accelerate your career or start a business, read this book."

Seymour Duncker, CEO and founder, iCharts

"Karen Kang lays out a powerful step-by-step system that makes personal branding actionable and achievable. Her stories and examples bring the methodology to life, and make the book a delight to read. I highly recommend BrandingPays for any professional serious about career success."

Larry Chang, President, Ascend Northern California,
and former Vice President of Finance, Global Supply Chain,
Hewlett-Packard

Branding Pays™

Branding

Pays™

The Five-Step
System to Reinvent
Your Personal Brand

Karen Kang

**BRANDING
PAYS**
MEDIA

BrandingPays Media books may be purchased
for educational, business or sales promotional use.

For information about copyright or bulk purchase,
contact BrandingPays Media at
BrandingPaysMedia@brandingpays.com,
855 El Camino Real, Suite 13A-157
Palo Alto, CA 94301-2326

Book design by
Leslie Guidice
Energy Energy Design

FIRST EDITION

Library of Congress Control Number: 2013931777

ISBN: 978-0-9884375-0-0

Ebook ISBN: 978-0-9884375-1-7

PRINTED IN THE UNITED STATES OF AMERICA

To Jon

Table of Contents

Foreword by Geoffrey Moore
Best-selling author of *Crossing the Chasm*

Chapter 3   60

Step 2: Messaging

Chapter 4   76

Step 3: Brand Strategy

Chapter 5   100

Step 4: Ecosystem

Chapter 6   122

Step 5: Action Plan

Chapter 7   142

360-Degree Branding: Vision, Symbols, Words and Deeds

Chapter 8   156

Portable Branding and Social Media: Getting Started

Foreword

As Karen Kang notes in her introduction, she and I were principals and later partners at Regis McKenna Inc. during the 1980s and early 1990s. This was a seminal time for high-tech marketing, and RMI was at the epicenter, in large part because Regis's book, *The Regis Touch,* laid out a whole new game plan for how to bring high-tech products to market.

Fast forward to 2013. This is another seminal time, this time for marketing "companies of one," or, more specifically, you. In the new business order, everyone is a contractor all the time. To be sure, you may at present be giving 100 percent of your capacity to a single client—your employer—but that in no way lessens your self-marketing responsibilities. Your boss is your primary client. Your colleagues are partners in your value chain. The company's customers are your customer's customers. And your job is to communicate to all these constituencies who you are, what you do, and why that is of value to them. Hence the rise of personal branding, and specifically what Karen calls "strategic personal branding."

This is not an exercise in egotism. In a funny way, this is not even about you. Rather, it is about establishing relationships within an ecosystem for the benefit of all participating. That is why Karen's experience at RMI is so relevant and valuable. This is what lay at the heart of redefining high-tech marketing. It was not about the product—it was about the *whole product,* the complete set of products and services that met the target customer's compelling reason to buy. Karen has taken this entire suite of intellectual property and further developed and repurposed it to serve a new constituency in a new era.

Your job is to embrace the challenge of personal branding and to leverage the models and methods this book lays out to position yourself to provide maximum value to others. That, in turn, will create maximum value for you, both in terms of personal fulfillment and financial success. But it is only available to those who step up to the self-marketing challenge. The new business order does not in general have time or patience to discover the real you. You must take the lead here, regardless of how extroverted or introverted you may be. It is simply part of your job.

BrandingPays gives you a comprehensive, proven approach to succeeding in this task. It was developed on behalf of start-ups and entrepreneurs, and that is how it asks you to think of yourself. As your teacher and cheerleader, Karen guides you every step of the way. With any luck, putting these practices to work will make for a better world and a happier you. To that end, you have my very best wishes.

Geoffrey Moore
Author, speaker, advisor

Introduction

The Importance of Reinventing Your Personal Brand

Personal branding—that is, creating your image and guiding your reputation—has never been more important than it is today. Why? Because globalization and social media have made the world smaller, more connected and infinitely more competitive. Your competition for a job or business opportunity may be anywhere in the world—at the desk next to you or continents away. It has never been more important to differentiate yourself from the pack.

My own corporate and personal branding business provides a great example of how everyone is competing for jobs and clients globally. Years ago, most of my service providers and clients were within a 20-mile radius of my Palo Alto, California, office. Today, I use a webmaster in Kuwait, a programming team in India and Los Angeles and a PR firm in Texas, and have clients in Asia, South America, Europe and throughout the United States. Word-of-mouth references are important, but so is one's web presence—being found by search engines and standing out in a crowded and noisy market.

In addition to global competition, there has been a tidal change in how new technologies have affected our businesses and lives. I now rely on such technologies as social media, web services for collaboration, cloud storage, videocasting, ebooks and webinars that were not in my vocabulary 10 years ago. Instead of listening to CDs and broadcast radio, I listen to music and podcasts on my iPhone or use a web music service. Instead of going to a brick-and-mortar bank, I use my smartphone for deposits, transfers and paying bills. In every industry, old ways of doing things are being replaced by new ways.

What does all this change mean for you? There is a tremendous opportunity to position your personal brand to take advantage of the shifts in the business landscape. It's not good enough to maintain the status quo. Just as businesses need to reinvent themselves for new markets, you need to reinvent yourself for new career opportunities. Pumping up the volume with a purely tactical approach may create awareness of your current brand, but it may not entice anyone to offer you a new opportunity.

You need to be strategic. Reinventing your brand for new opportunities requires an understanding of market forces, your own assets and how you need to be positioned in the new world order. Think of yourself as a free agent—no one else is looking out for your best interests but yourself. You need to be crystal clear about who you are and the value you bring to a world where constant change is the only norm.

If you want to stay competitive, you need to ask: Do I have a personal brand that gives me an advantage in today's world?

In short, brand yourself, or be left behind.

Anyone Can Master Personal Branding

Personal branding is not rocket science. Creating the image that defines your unique value is something anyone can master. It's not just the purview of branding gurus and social media mavens.

Unfortunately, few understand what it takes to build a strong brand—online or offline. Some may be defeating themselves by promoting a weak image and a me-too message to an audience that doesn't care.

The best companies go through a rigorous process to develop the strategy to market and brand their products. But, as individuals, we often lack the understanding, the process or the tools to develop a strong brand strategy. I wrote *BrandingPays™: The Five-Step System to Reinvent Your Personal Brand* to fill this need. The focus of it is on building a brand positioning strategy and developing your image and key messages, but it also includes many practical tips for implementation.

I want to help you feel confident in branding yourself. Personal branding is a skill that will pay huge dividends throughout your life and career.

What's Inside *BrandingPays*

BrandingPays: The Five-Step System to Reinvent Your Personal Brand is an excellent guide for:

- Professionals who want to get a job or new position, change careers or get promoted

- Recent graduates looking for a new job or position

- Entrepreneurs who need to brand both themselves and their companies

The book lays out the practical BrandingPays Five-Step System for personal branding. This methodology makes branding as easy to understand as "Bake the cake, then ice it," a metaphor I use to talk about the rational value (cake) and emotional value (icing) that make up strong brands.

I've highlighted lessons and examples from my 20-plus years of branding experience and included insightful anecdotes and case histories from both companies and individuals. The book is filled with templates, graphic examples, action lists and URLs for online resources.

Throughout this book, I've included examples and stories based on real people. In most cases, I've used pseudonyms and changed some identifying circumstances to protect their identities. A few of the examples are composites.

Since our brands will change over time, we all need to be good at refreshing them. Use this book as a reference throughout your career to reinvent yourself for new opportunities.

Chapter Focus

Chapter 1 defines personal branding and introduces concepts that will help you to get more out of the BrandingPays System. This chapter introduces the cake-and-icing metaphor to help make branding more understandable. We'll have fun looking at celebrity brands and start you thinking about your own cake and icing.

Chapter 2 through Chapter 6 lay out the BrandingPays System. A chapter is devoted to each of the five steps.

Chapter 7 looks at how to implement a 360-degree brand.

Chapter 8 examines the fundamentals of social branding and how you can guide your brand when you can't always control how others represent you visually or through words.

My Story

I'd like to share my story with you in the hope that you will be inspired to develop your own brand. At the end of this book, I've also included a number of inspirational stories of people who have succeeded in business and personal branding in spite of being seen as outliers.

My roots are humble. I am a Korean American who grew up on a small family farm. In the early 1900s, my grandfather was recruited from Korea to work the sugar cane fields in Hawaii. My grandmother, from whom I got my independent nature, ran away from her affluent home in Pusan, Korea, to escape an arranged marriage. When her audacious dream of a university education did not pan out, she became a "picture bride" to my grandfather, a perfect stranger.

My dad was a high school dropout with tough-guy tendencies and my mom was a well-read and artistic soul. (I guess opposites attract!) They were an unlikely couple to become farmers, something they knew nothing about. But it was hard to say no to my grandmother, the one-time picture bride and family matriarch. She believed that Dad, who was a pushover beneath his bad-boy image, should leave his job as a merchant seaman and buy a farm in Oregon for a better life for his young family. And so it was.

As a family, we planted and hoed cabbage fields, picked strawberries and tended to our sometimes struggling farm. For entertainment, I grew up playing with mud pies and exploring the backwoods. We had riding horses, but there were no ballets, no operas or violin concertos in our provincial lives. We were a happy family, but I dreamed of a life beyond our little farm.

When I was seventeen, I got a scholarship to attend Mills College, a private all-women's college, in Oakland, California, which I later learned was where my mother had hoped to go to school. What I loved about Mills, beyond its proximity to the cultural delights of San Francisco, was its diverse community and the philosophy that women could become whatever they wanted. Mills encouraged me to follow my passion and make a difference in the world. This belief has become the bedrock for my personal brand.

You could argue that I am the poster child for reinventing one's personal brand. I started my career with newspaper journalism jobs beginning with an internship at a newspaper in Paris (France) during my junior year abroad. I did a stint as a reporter at *The (Portland) Oregonian* soon after graduation from Mills. Hoping to land a reporting job on the East Coast, I attended Boston University's graduate program in journalism. My BU degree and Oregonian clip file helped me to get a newspaper reporting job just outside of Boston. I must have done a good job of branding myself because, to my knowledge, I was the only one in my Master's program who had a job offer at graduation. (However, my BU colleagues did get journalism jobs later).

Returning to California after two years in Boston, I participated in the exciting growth of high tech marketing as a practitioner and later as an executive with agencies for public relations and advertising. I helped launch new companies and positioned them for successful initial public offerings (like Maxtor, which is now a Seagate brand), introduced industry-changing technologies and participated in creating new markets. Each time I changed jobs, I had to reposition myself to be seen of value to my new employers. For example. I have positioned myself at various times as a former journalist turned PR pro, a PR exec who could sell new programs to advertising clients, an ad agency exec with integrated marketing leadership, and a marketing strategist who could bridge strategies to implementation. Today, through my client work and social media reputation, I am positioned as a brand strategist for corporate and personal branding.

Building on the Thought Leadership of Regis McKenna and Geoffrey Moore

My real fortune was being hired by Regis McKenna Inc. (RMI), the eponymous firm of the marketing and brand guru, which did landmark brand positioning for Apple, Intel and Genentech. My orientation included being embedded in RMI's Apple account team to learn first-hand the secrets of an Apple product launch. Many of these proven techniques—such as positioning, messaging and influencer (ecosystem) briefings—have been optimized for personal branding in the BrandingPays™ System. To prove that nothing is new under the sun, I have built upon these techniques as well as the positioning and relationship marketing concepts that were originally conceived by Regis McKenna, a true marketing visionary.

During my six years doing strategy consulting at RMI as a principal and partner, I enjoyed working with many of the best and the brightest consultants and clients. One of the RMI partners was Geoffrey Moore, the best-selling author of the marketing classic *Crossing the Chasm*. Geoff and I teamed on a number of strategy consulting projects at RMI. I am happy to say I'm still learning from him during our friendly breakfasts at Buck's in Woodside, California.

One of the most dramatic rebranding examples in my life occurred during my venture into the Italian vacation business in 2004. During a two-year hiatus from Silicon Valley marketing consulting, I became co-founder and president of an Italian vacation company (our tagline: "Savor the Real Italy"). I immersed myself in everything Italian—language, culture, fashion, food and travel—and became trusted as an Italy expert among friends and potential clients. Building a successful brand in Italian travel taught me that personal branding and company branding are synergistic, especially if you are an entrepreneur.

I came back to consulting because, as a recent entrepreneur, I wanted to help other entrepreneurs understand the importance and power of branding their businesses and themselves. I created the BrandingPays System first for companies, but soon understood its applicability to people. The fact that I work with both companies and individuals is a plus. I can bring the discipline of corporate branding to individuals and the consumer and social media insights from personal branding to companies.

Over my career, I've consulted to or trained more than 150 companies—from Fortune 500 to start-up firms—and thousands of professionals on developing a compelling brand. The BrandingPays System has helped many individuals get their dream job or accelerate their career success. My dream is that all professionals learn both the art and science of personal branding, because it will yield dividends throughout their lifetime.

Personal branding is not as easy as filling in the blanks. If you truly want to stand out, you will have to be aware of your environment (the market, the trends and the competitive opportunities) and think critically about what assets you have and how to leverage them to your advantage. If you are willing to put in the time and effort, you will be richly rewarded. A strong personal brand can help you get a job, a promotion, investor funding or new clients.

Your brand is arguably your most important asset. Isn't it worth investing in?

Take Charge of
Your Personal Brand

Branding a Political Candidate

After residing in Palo Alto for seven years, Hillary Freeman decided to run for City Council in her California hometown. A devoted wife, soccer mom and public schools volunteer, Hillary worked as a high-tech sales executive in Silicon Valley. Having moved to Palo Alto from Los Angeles, she loved the character and charm of her adopted city.

However, Hillary had a challenge. Home to Stanford University, Palo Alto was a community of well-educated, high-income and predominantly white citizens. Blacks represented less than 2 percent of the population at the time—and Hillary Freeman is African American.

Although politically progressive, Palo Alto, like any place, was not immune to racial prejudice. At a Hillary Freeman campaign event early in the race, for instance, a newspaper photographer took her photo and, thinking she was a volunteer and not the candidate, asked where she lived.

"Palo Alto," she replied.

"You mean *East* Palo Alto," he said, since many believed the only blacks in town were from East Palo Alto, a neighboring town that had a reputation for drug-related violence.

In order to meet her goal, Hillary needed to get past racial stereotypes and the fact that she had no political experience. Working with her as the campaign strategist, we created a brand that positioned her as the face of new leadership in Palo Alto—a high-tech exec whose business skills and empathy could align city policies with community values. Hillary, her campaign team and I strategized to match Hillary's unique strengths with the needs of the community. We paired the critical issues facing Palo Alto with the need for a City Council member who had a business background to tackle budget issues, along with the values of a mom with school-age children (education, libraries and sports fields) and a homeowner concerned about balancing the needs of development with neighborhood character. We built a coalition of stakeholders who were invested in her success because her campaign spoke to their needs and vision for Palo Alto. By focusing on shared values and her education (BA and MS degrees), Hillary seemed like "one of us" and not a black outsider.

During the campaign, Hillary went from being an unknown minority volunteer to an exciting candidate who best represented Palo Alto ideals. The results of Hillary's campaign and brand transformation were stunning. She not only won a seat on the City Council, but also was the highest vote-getter in a field of 13, besting two incumbents and ousting the sitting mayor. Hillary had to overcome seemingly insurmountable odds to reach her goal. She is living proof that branding does pay.

What Is Personal Branding?

"What does a political race have to do with personal branding and my goal of getting a job or investor funding?" you may ask. Whether competing in politics, in the job market or against other entrepreneurs, you need to stand out and prove that you are the best choice—just like a political candidate.

> **The perfect storm of extreme competition for jobs and the explosion of social media has propelled personal branding from a "nice to have" to a "got to do."**

For professionals, a strong personal brand is the key to influence, opportunities and advancement. For recent graduates, personal brands can be the difference between getting a job and ending up in the circular file. For entrepreneurs, a personal brand that inspires confidence can be the edge that propels investors to fund you.

Yet many people haven't a clue as to what personal branding is or what to do to achieve a brand. Many think that personal branding is merely cosmetic. There's a saying that goes, "You can put lipstick on a pig, but it's still a pig." This is true of personal branding. You can put on a new suit, but if you lack substance or content, people will see the makeover for what it is—shallow and lacking real proof of change.

Regis McKenna, Silicon Valley brand guru and my former boss, put it best when he told me in a recent email:

My concern is that "personal branding" only works if there is valued content. Example, when Steve Jobs left [Apple] he was often compared to Adam Osborne and Nolan Bushnell—people who blew it. His credibility was zero as far as personal computing was concerned even after he rejoined Apple in 1998. People only sat up and took notice when the iMac (the multi-colored editions) took off and Apple returned to growth and profitability.

Profitability and growth are the two best marketing programs a company or its leader can use to gain leadership. You may recall that I used to quote Tevye from *Fiddler on the Roof*. "If I were a rich man, I would sit in the temple and lecture to the wise man all day long and it wouldn't matter if you know or not, when you're rich, they think you know."

I can't agree with him more. When you have the goods, it's a lot easier to brand yourself and to get recognized. But having the goods isn't all. You need to position what you have to your best competitive advantage.

What if you are just starting out, or if you are weak on evidence that sets you apart? Mia is an example of how you can build your evidence from scratch. Hers may not be the model for everyone, but it does demonstrate how far you can go with strong aptitude and hard work. Mia got her college degree in theater and had thought she wanted to be an actress. However, after taking a career aptitude test, she decided she was better suited to a career in web design and development. Luckily for her, new web programming standards meant that her learning curve was not that much steeper than that for experienced developers.

Mia self-studied with the latest web programming books and spent six months writing sample programs with the help of an experienced mentor. When she felt ready, she priced her services right and got a contracting job in web development with a small professional services firm. As she worked to build her portfolio, she positioned herself on LinkedIn as a front-end web developer with strong consumer understanding (from her retail jobs and acting) and artistic sensibility (evidenced by her theater design and art background). Her LinkedIn profile attracted job recruiters and she landed a full-time job with a mobile web software start-up doing customer-facing web development—the cool interactive stuff you see on mobile screens. Even if you have little to work with, you can dramatically reinvent your brand the way Mia did with hard work, smart positioning and a little help from some friends.

We've touched on the concept of personal branding, but let's make sure we are on the same page in how we define it. Think of personal branding as both what you create (your personal brand) and the act of creating it.

A personal brand is your image and reputation.

Whether you like it or not, you already have a personal brand. The world perceives you in a particular way and puts you in certain categories. From an external imaging standpoint, what you wear, your personality, and your gestures and presence guide how people perceive you. But, more importantly, your unique knowledge and experience (e.g., mobile technology licensing or change management) is the foundation of your brand value.

> ## Are you known for something of value, or are you a victim of others branding you?

For instance, perhaps you need to reinvent your brand from:

- Doer to leader
- Inexperienced graduate to a professional with 21st-century skills
- Technology geek to technology business CEO

If your current brand will not get you to the next level of your career or the next business opportunity, you need to change your brand.

Personal branding is the act of developing the strategy and actions to guide your brand.

What should you be saying and doing to represent your brand the way you want?

> ## Without a brand goal, strategy and action plan, personal branding becomes akin to baking a cake without a recipe.

You may hope for a three-tiered masterpiece but end up with an inedible concoction. With a good strategy and action plan, you can create a personal brand that makes the world want to hire, promote or fund you.

Personal Branding Myths

Do you maintain beliefs that are hindering your ability to create a strong personal brand? You are not alone. Many people hold onto the following misguided beliefs:

1. Doing great work = a great reputation
2. My boss will market my brand
3. Self-promotion is boastful and bad

We need to dispel these myths so that you can start on your personal branding journey without being sabotaged by a brand-hindering belief system.

Myth #1: Doing great work = a great reputation

You've been slaving away at your job. You have worked weekends, woken at the crack of dawn to finish the report your boss requested the night before, delivered on your objectives and your numbers—all without complaint. Surely, you will be recognized for your sacrifice and productivity.

At the department meeting on Monday morning, your boss will announce a new promotion. You start writing your acceptance speech and thinking of whom you will thank for helping you achieve this recognition. *But, what, say that again?* Kyle is the new director. How can that be? Kyle is a lightweight. He does not consistently make his numbers. He spends more time schmoozing than doing real work. *You've been robbed!*

I've heard so many variations on this theme—from professionals around the world. Why does my company take me for granted? How can I get the reputation and rewards that I deserve?

People are not mind readers. They have no way of knowing what great work you are doing unless you let them know. You have to market your contributions to be recognized for your value.

The next two myths are variations on the same theme.

Myth #2: My boss will market my brand

John had had a stellar career in advertising. He followed his boss from company to company, where John was promoted and given more responsibilities and a larger salary with every move. When his boss retired, John's biggest cheerleader was gone. John lacked his own personal brand and network, and could not get the jobs that he wanted. John needed to be his own brand manager and not rely solely on his boss to brand him.

Certain cultures cultivate the image of the boss as a paternal figure who looks after your welfare. For this reason, many Asians in my seminars say that they think it is the job of their boss to market their value. Every individual needs to understand that in today's economy, you have to be responsible for your own destiny. The era of the paternalistic company or boss is over. Even Japanese companies, who historically never laid off workers, are adopting workforce reduction policies to stay flexible and competitive.

Know that your boss is busy. She has too much to do to prioritize promoting your brand. What if she leaves the company? All the equity you built with this one person will walk out the door when she leaves.

> **Don't be a victim. Be your own brand manager.**

To be considered for a new job, a new opportunity or investor funding, you have to be known. Leaving the branding to others is losing control over your brand. Would you rather brand yourself or let your competitors brand you? The choice should be clear.

Myth # 3: Self-promotion is boastful and bad

Most people do not like promoting themselves because of cultural barriers or a personal preference to stay in the background. If you were taught from a young age that you should be humble, then marketing your achievements seems to fly in the face of your cultural values.

At one of my personal branding seminars, an accomplished but quiet Chinese manager named Mary told me that all of her life she was taught humility and deference to your elders or boss were important values. For this reason, she never spoke up in meetings and never called attention to herself. I advised her to:

- Own a place at the table. Know and act like you belong there. Don't just take up space. You need to contribute your good ideas and show value.

- Share your work or achievements with your boss and group as a means of educating them about new ideas or best practices.

A few months later, Mary told me I had "changed her life." The branding work helped her to position her unique value and to have the confidence to contribute at strategy meetings. The result was that her boss chose her to lead a key business team.

Self-promotion should not be an exercise in boasting, which can be off-putting. Education is a better concept. Brand education helps a target audience to recognize your value. In the case of Mary, communicating her strategic capabilities helped her to be considered for a leadership role that had eluded her in the past.

Promotion is often thought of as one-way communication from the sender to the receiver. We need to engage in two-way communication and value.

> **When communication flows both ways, brands are more engaging and memorable.**

For instance, when you post interesting content and engage in online conversations with followers, the interaction lets you build your brand without being boastful.

If you still feel you can't educate the world on your brand for your own benefit, then do it for your organization. If you have a stronger and more valued brand, it will enhance your organization's brand. If no one knows about your unique value, the world loses out on your experience, expertise and opportunities to engage.

> **Self-promotion, therefore, is really about educating the market about your value.**

Figure 1.1

What Are the Benefits of Personal Branding?

When you are able to articulate your unique brand value, you will be rewarded in a number of ways.

Respect. Your name will have a certain cachet. Your reputation will grow.

Ecosystem will advocate for you. Influencers will make introductions or endorse you.

Opportunities will arise, such as jobs, clients, projects, partnerships, and speaking and media opportunities.

Success. You will land the job, climb the career ladder or get funding for your company.

Enjoy work and life. By living your desired brand, you will feel more fulfilled at work and in life.

In short, life is better with a great brand.

Rebranding Throughout Life

We live in a world where constant change presents both opportunities and challenges for branding. Google and Facebook, two companies that have redefined our culture and the business world, did not exist before 1996 and 2004, respectively. However, today the Internet browser has become *the* platform for communications, sharing and services. I know of many professionals and entrepreneurs who were slow to rebrand for the opportunities afforded by this shift in technology and business model, and they suffered the consequences.

The world is dynamic. Your brand needs to change with the times. According to the Bureau of Labor Statistics, an average worker may have multiple careers and hold more than ten different jobs during his or her lifetime. Here are six key changes that may trigger a need to refresh your brand:

- New job search or career change

- Change in company ownership, leadership, your assignment or your boss

- Change in cultural values (customer-centric, one team, innovation, etc.)

- Shift in desired leadership traits (cross-functional, global, collaborative, flexible, etc.)

- Shift in technology or business strategy

- Reduction in workforce

Strategically managing your personal brand will help you to be proactive and in charge of your career. The BrandingPays™ System has concepts and tools to help you refresh your brand throughout your lifetime.

Your Goal for Branding

The BrandingPays System works best when you have a goal. You won't know if you have succeeded in branding if you don't define what you are trying to achieve. The Branding Journey (Figure 1.2) is a way to look at the stages of personal branding that lead to a strong brand. Everyone wants his or her brand to be recognized and preferred. But starting at the end is putting the cart before the horse. You need to know where you are headed before you set branding in motion—otherwise, you may be going nowhere fast. The starting point in personal branding is having a goal and a strategy to achieve it. Your goal can be as simple as being recognized for your unique value in your current job. Or it may be landing a new job, changing careers or getting funding for your company. If you don't have a specific goal today, don't worry; the BrandingPays System can help you to identify new opportunities and potential goals.

Figure 1.2

The Branding Journey
Where are you on the journey?

Look at this chart and determine where you are on the journey to a strong personal brand. Ask yourself the questions below.

Goal, strategy and messages	*Do I have a clear goal, strategy and messages to achieve the brand I want?* You need to know where you want to go. Then, you have to develop the positioning, messaging, brand strategy and influencer understanding to get there.
Brand evidence	*Do I have evidence of both the cake (rational value) and icing (emotional value) for a strong brand?* Figure out what areas you will need to invest in to create your desired brand and deliver on your unique value. You need to be your brand.
Brand relationships	*Do I have meaningful relationships with key influencers who affect my success?* You need to develop relationships with key individuals who influence opinions both through social media and in person.
Brand education	*Do I communicate my brand effectively and deliver on a consistent brand experience through my image, personality, messages and actions?* If you have a brand that others like, value and endorse, you have a strong brand. Having a credible and visible brand will help you achieve your dreams faster—in both your life and career.

If you've answered "no" to most of the questions, don't despair. Follow the steps in this book to accelerate your branding journey.

Every Brand Needs Cake and Icing

We brand people every day in our minds and in what we say to others. *Raj is the go-to marketing expert. Helen is the brilliant strategist. Soo is the office social director. Carl is the company misanthrope.*

What are people saying about you?

If it's not what you want, you can change it. Branding is not just for brand gurus. You can be your own brand expert. You just have to "bake the cake, then ice it."

You may wonder what a cake has to do with branding. The cake is just a metaphor to help us understand what branding is all about. Think of the iced cake as your brand.

Figure 1.3
Bake the Cake, then Ice It

Cake = Your rational value
Functional benefits, expertise

Icing = Your emotional value
Personality, image

CAKE + ICING = STRONG BRAND

- The cake foundation represents the *rational value* for your brand—your expertise, strengths, functional value and experience.

- The icing is your *emotional value*—your personality, your smile and your style. It's how people connect with you emotionally, such as your likability and whether they trust you.

To be a strong brand, you need to have both cake and icing. You need to marry the rational with the emotional.

You've probably met people who appeared to be all icing and no cake. For instance, our first impression when seeing a beautiful supermodel might be that she is all icing. Then there are people who appear to be all cake and no icing, the stereotype for most engineers. You need to achieve a balance.

Let's look at a consumer brand example to help us better understand the role of cake and icing. Starbucks is a leading café and coffee brand. Starbucks' cake, or rational value, is providing a consistently good cup of coffee. The icing, or emotional value, is providing an inviting gathering place, friendly baristas, support for worthy causes and, for some, a brand that introduces us to new music. Starbucks has many competitors, but few have its rational and emotional brand power.

It's easy to see how consumer products are branded, but how does the branding of people work? Before we take a look at you, let's look at people who are more sophisticated in the care and feeding of their brands—that is, celebrities.

©Alberto E. Rodriguez/
Getty Images Entertainment/Getty Images

When you look at this picture of actor George Clooney, what is the first thing that comes to mind?

"He's a talented actor and director." That's cake.

"He's a handsome and charming guy." That's icing.

"He's a humanitarian activist." That's both cake (rational value as a humanitarian) and icing (emotional value as someone who cares).

We can go through quick associations for other celebrities like Kim Kardashian (cake=reality star and icing=beauty), Hillary Clinton (cake=Secretary of State and icing=personable and caring) and Bono (cake=rock singer and icing=humanitarian who cares).

What we associate with people can be both good and bad. You might say that you know of people who have reputations as being jerks, but they are still successful. I can think of a number of CEOs who demoralize employees by belittling them. These company leaders will ride high as long as they deliver bottom-line results.

But when they no longer produce the expected results, these CEOs, whose negative icing outweighs the positive cake, become vulnerable.

Let's leave the celebrity realm and move closer to your reality. What are the personal brands that you admire in your profession? What is the cake and what is the icing of those who are successful?

See Figure 1.4 for a chart of some personal brands for professionals. Try to articulate what you think your cake and icing are. You'll be able to compare this to your Brand Strategy Platform that we'll develop later in Chapter 6.

Figure 1.4

Cake and Icing Examples

Examples	Cake (rational value)	Icing (emotional value)
Software Engineer	Open software leader	Sense of humor, geek chic style
Marketing Executive	Social Media Marketing expert	Charismatic, hip, positive attitude
Founder and CEO	Technology guru, Business vision	Inspirational, caring non-profit volunteer
YOU	?	?

Eileen, a product marketing director who consistently delivered great marketing programs, wanted to become a vice president at her company. Her boss recognized that her hard-charging approach produced results, but new management was changing the company culture to one that valued leaders with collaboration skills and emotional intelligence. Eileen lacked evidence of collaborative leadership skills (cake) and empathy (icing). She is now working on being recognized for new cake and icing that will move her closer to a leadership brand that the company will value.

> **The better you understand your current brand, the easier it will be to develop a strategy to change it for the better.**

Perhaps your company does 360 assessments of what your boss, peers and reports think of your management capability, leadership style and performance. Take a look at these assessments and note common themes—both good and bad. The themes can help you to understand how others view you and inventory your assets and liabilities. These perceptions will provide valuable input to your thinking as you develop your positioning and brand strategy.

If you don't have 360 review data or want to supplement existing assessments, you can use the BrandingPays questions (see Figure 1.5) that are geared to provide input to the brand positioning process. These questions can be sent to those who know you well professionally. Go to www.brandingpays.com/resources to download the personal brand assessment questions.

Figure 1.5A

Personal Branding Assessment Questionnaire

I'm working on a personal branding exercise and would value your candid input. Please answer the questions below as best you can. Short, bulleted answers are fine. I've included a sample list of Brand Attribute ideas to spark your thinking.

1. Core values

   - What do you think my core values are?

2. Key strengths and weaknesses

   - What is my key skill set?
   - What is my expertise?
   - What are the weaknesses that may hold me back?

3. Unique value proposition

   - What is my unique expertise or value that differentiates me?

4. Personality/image attributes

   - How do I come across to others?
   - What are the key adjectives that describe my personality?
   - Describe my look and style.

5. Leadership attributes

- What kind of a leader am I?

6. Relationship attributes

- What is it like to engage with me—professionally and socially?

7. What is a living or inanimate thing that best represents my brand? Please explain. Examples:

- A trusted Saint Bernard dog who always come to the rescue
- A Mini Cooper car that is efficient, fun to drive and has a quirky sense of style

---

The following list of potential brand attributes may help to spur ideas as you answer the questions above.

Figure 1.5B

Sample Brand Attributes

Core Values	Strengths	Personality	Image
• Trust	• Project management	• Visionary	• Sophisticated
• Courage	• People management	• Positive	• Elegant
• Respect	• Financial or operations management	• Strategic	• Edgy
• Integrity	• Technical expertise	• Creative	• Buttoned-down
• Passion	• Strategic planning	• Present	• Classic
• Innovation	• Managing conflict	• Focused	• Business casual
• Transparency	• Creative problem solving	• Flexible	• Fashion forward
• Adaptability	• Delivering presentations	• Inspirational	• Urban
• Reliability	• Decision making	• Sense of humor	• Artistic
• Accountability	• Mentoring	• Compassionate	• Establishment
• Honesty	• Communication	• Patient	• Couture
• Giving back	• Strategic vision	• Results-oriented	• Technology savvy
• Leadership	• Collaboration & teamwork	• Analytical	• Worldly
• Vision	• Building and leading teams	• Confident	• Cultured
• Quality	• Leading innovation	• Competent	• Hip
• Diversity	• Global strategies	• Expert	• Colorful
• Thought leadership	• Streamlining processes	• Unflappable	• Conservative
• Service	• Domain expertise	• Driven	• Academic
• Helping others	• Driving for results	• Passionate	• Professional
• Education	• Change management	• Collaborative	• Geek chic
• Competence		• Personable	• Entrepreneurial
• Respect		• Energetic	• Leader
• Responsibility		• Friendly	• (see Personality list)
• Open mind			
• Friendship			
• Determination			

To access PDF version, go to www.brandingpays.com/resources

Are there any themes that have emerged from the answers you've received? For instance, have people described you as "adaptable," "flexible" and "agile"? If so, the consistent theme is the ability to adapt to changes, which is a highly desirable trait in business. You will want to include this in your branding as you move through the chapters of this book.

The BrandingPays System
Five Steps to Your Cake and Icing

Now that you better understand yourself and how others think of you, how do you shape your brand? The BrandingPays™ System (Figure 1.6) includes all the steps you need to take to figure out your cake and icing and communicate it to the world.

Figure 1.6

The BrandingPays Five-Step System

- Step 1: Positioning (Chapter 2). Define your unique cake, or rational value.

- Step 2: Messages (Chapter 3). Develop the key messages that support your cake.

- Step 3: Brand Strategy (Chapter 4). Put your cake and icing together in the Brand Strategy Platform. You will brand from the inside out for an authentic, 360-degree brand.

- Step 4: Ecosystem (Chapter 5). Define the influencer model for your brand ecosystem, and develop a strategy for relationship building and management. (Think of this as a distribution and reference model for your cake and icing.)

- Step 5: Action Plan (Chapter 6). Develop an action plan that includes 1) brand improvement for both your cake and icing and 2) brand communication so your brand can be known and recognized.

You might think, "I don't have time to do a strategy. I just want to do something now." Most of us want to start with tactics. Implementing something feels like we're taking action. It's the reason why millions of professionals are flocking to social media—often without a clue as to why.

> **Posting on social media or going to more networking events without a clear strategy is an example of "hurry up and wait."**

You'll get out there faster, but if the world isn't clear on what value your brand delivers, then the confusion you create will only serve to slow adoption of your brand.

Therefore, starting with tactics is like icing your cake before you bake it. The icing will not stand on its own without a cake foundation. You need to know what you want to be known for. You need to have a branding goal and strategy. Few of us, however, understand how to do this. This book will give you the framework and tools to create a strong brand that helps you achieve your goals.

BrandingPays is about taking charge of your personal brand and not leaving it up to chance. You don't have to be a victim of your circumstances or how others have branded you in the past. In writing this book, I hope to inspire you and empower you to take action to better your brand.

Positioning

Step 1: Positioning
◎ ◎ ◎ ◎ ◎

Position Yourself for Opportunities

Bob and Mike are software programmers in their fifties. Years ago, they were both at the top of their field in graphics software for the desktop.
Bob was confident his programming skills that got him to where he was today would carry him through to retirement. He was wrong. The technology landscape changed with mobile and browser-based computing. He was laid off from his job and could not find a new one because he was branded as "old school."

Mike, however, constantly kept a sharp eye on maintaining his unique value to his field—that is, his cake. At different intervals in his career, he asked, "What are the big-picture trends in the industry, in technology and in my company? What can I do to take advantage of changes in my environment?" Mike learned about new technologies, developed relationships with leading technologists and gained a reputation as a visionary. When it came time to look for a new job, he got two excellent offers from leading technology companies.

Today, Mike is recognized at his company and in the industry as a leader in graphical web software. Unlike Bob, who is unemployed, Mike positioned himself for new opportunities.

What Is Positioning and Why Do It?

When people think of personal branding, they might think wardrobe, mannerisms and catch phrases that others can remember. These, however, are just the finishing touches—or icing on the cake. Effective personal branding goes much deeper. It starts with positioning—your cake foundation, or rational value.

What Is Your Goal?

Before defining your positioning, let's identify your career or opportunity goal. Having such a goal is very important in personal branding. If you have a career goal, it will help to guide you in making choices about your desired brand.

If you are currently a director and want to become a vice president, perhaps you will have to position yourself from a group leader to an effective company leader. Think back to Eileen, the marketing director who wanted to be promoted to vice president. She needed to demonstrate not only her strategic leadership capability, but also her ability to align her personal brand values with the company's new culture.

Unless they are self-funded, entrepreneurs need to find investors who believe in their companies to reach their dreams. Their goal is not getting a job; it is getting the company funded. Entrepreneurs have to understand what investors value and position their companies in a way that meets investor needs.

Often MBA students are getting their degree with the hope of switching careers, say from hardware engineering to marketing. If you are an engineer, your first goal out of the MBA program should not be a consumer marketing position. It's just too great a leap of faith to go from being a hardware engineer to, say, marketing breakfast cereals. It would make more sense to set your sights on a marketing job at a technology company where you could leverage your engineering background.

When choosing your goals, you need to be somewhat realistic. Doing a 180-degree turn in personality or skill set is difficult to achieve. Let's say your goal is to become a company CEO but you are shy and feel uncomfortable speaking in public. Either your goal needs to change or your personality needs an overhaul, because shyness and feeling ill at ease speaking publicly is not a winning combination for being a CEO. You might consider altering your career goal to something that is more within reach.

Positioning Triangulation

One way to figure out your positioning goal is to explore the options through triangulation (Figure 2.1). That's just a fancy term for a three-pronged model to understand whether there is an audience (an employer, a boss, a venture capitalist or a client) that values what you have to offer. This is basically what we do in positioning, but the triangulation model helps with understanding the dependencies. By iterating different scenarios in the triangulation model, you will find the best option for you before writing your positioning statement.

Figure 2.1

Triangulation Model

What category can you lead?

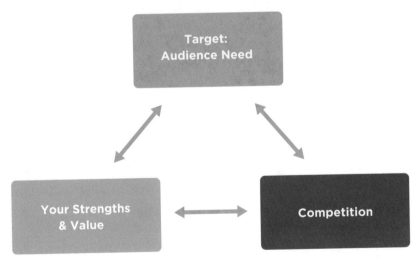

Remember Hillary Freeman, who wanted a seat on the Palo Alto City Council? The target audience need we identified was that many Palo Alto voters wanted new leadership and passion for their values. Hillary's strengths and values were that she was a high-tech business executive who had demonstrated community values as a community and schools volunteer leader. We established that there was a need for a candidate with Hillary's strengths and values, but then we had to see if other candidates (her competition) could fulfill the audience need. Her opportunity was that few, if any, candidates demonstrated her passion and grass-roots support across key constituencies: schools, library lovers, youth sports, YMCA and neighborhood groups. If we found that other candidates had the same messages and evidence that Hillary had, we would have had to change Hillary's positioning goal.

Figure 2.2

Sample Triangulation

Hillary Freeman Has a Competitive Positioning Opportunity

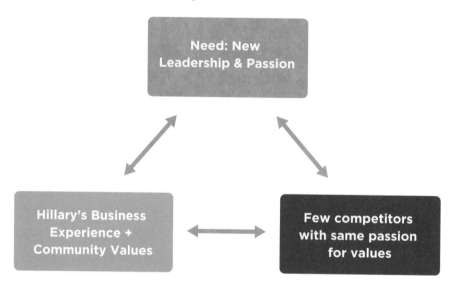

Pamela is another interesting example. She had spent the last few years as a marketing director for a drug company and had excellent credentials building her product brands and growing the business. However, she wanted to move away from marketing and get into the area of her passion: ensuring patient access to health care—specifically, her company's therapeutic drugs. The good news was that there was less competition in this area versus marketing, and her graduate degree from a school of public health helped to distinguish her. The target audience need was real in that her company had significant resources dedicated to patient access and cared about this area. In the end, she positioned herself as an accomplished health care executive and patient access expert. With clarity on her goal and value, she had the confidence to have a frank talk with her boss about her career path.

The result? Her company created a new job for her that was tailored to her passions and talents. Within six months on the job, she was promoted to senior director. Pamela is an excellent example of how to best differentiate yourself for an opportunity by optimizing the triangulation of target audience need, your strengths and value, and competition.

Positioning Statement

The triangulation exercise has prepared you for writing your positioning statement, the first step in the BrandingPays System. This statement is a tool to help you to ensure that you have a unique and compelling value proposition for a particular target audience.

Remember that we "bake the cake, then ice it." The cake is your positioning. This is the foundation for a strong brand. Without it, your brand would be all fluff, or icing—not very substantial or credible.

> **The positioning statement provides the foundation for developing your elevator pitch and key value messages for different audiences.**

It will also provide input to the Brand Strategy Platform (chapter 4), where we put your cake and icing together.

Despite popular belief, your positioning statement is not your elevator pitch. Elements of your positioning statement, however, will be used in your elevator pitch and key messages, which we'll explore in chapter 3.

See Figure 2.3 for our positioning statement template. There are five positioning elements that we need to consider:

- Target Audience

- Problem Statement

- Category

- Value Proposition

- Competitive Differentiation

Figure 2.3

Positioning Statement

Target Audience	For...
Problem Statement	Who needs or wants...
Category	I am...
Value Proposition	Who provides...
Competitive Differentiation	Unlike...

Geoffrey Moore, the author of *Crossing the Chasm* and a fellow Regis McKenna partner, did the business world a great service when he developed the positioning statement format that is basically a run-on sentence that goes:

For (target audience)
Who needs or wants (problem statement)
Our product is a (category)
That (value proposition)
Unlike (key competitor), our product is . . . (competitive differentiation)

The beauty of this format is that it is a great way to ensure you understand your audience's needs and message your value in a compelling way.

When applied to personal branding, you are the "product" in the positioning statement.

> **Thinking of yourself as a product may help you to see yourself and your opportunities objectively.**

Who Is Your Target Audience?

It's important to have a distinct audience in mind because otherwise you will try to be all things to all people, and your positioning will be too general and undifferentiated.

Think about your target audience first. Who are they? If your goal is to land a great job with a hot new company, that company, your future boss and the HR team are your target audiences. If you're working toward a promotion or new position in your current company, your would-be boss or group executive is your target audience. If you are an entrepreneur looking for venture capital, your prospective venture capitalists represent your target audiences.

What if you have different audiences with different needs? You can always write different positioning statements to help you message to the different audiences. However, your overall positioning category should remain the same if your target audiences talk to one another. You need to put a stake in the ground to be known for something. It's understandable if you position differently for different job opportunities, but once in a job, keep your positioning the same until you decide to change for strategic reasons. If you flit from one positioning category to another, your positioning will be unclear. People will not consider you for opportunities without a clear understanding of how you are positioned to add value.

Problem or Opportunity Statement: What do *they* need?

In positioning, we are either solving a problem or enabling an opportunity. Sometimes it's both.

In defining the problem statement, ask: What is the main problem my target audience faces? What are their challenges that I can address? Only when you understand these well can you start to position yourself as part of the solution. Otherwise you might be a perfect solution, but to the wrong problem—a problem your target audience doesn't happen to have.

Do you recall Eileen, our product marketing director who wanted to be promoted as a vice president? She chose her boss, the Senior VP of Marketing, as her target audience. However, her target audience should have been the executive leadership team who would have to promote her as a peer, and whose needs were different from the pain points of the VP of Marketing. By choosing the wrong target audience, her positioning strategy for becoming a vice president would be less effective. As Eileen's example points out, the target audience, problem statement and value proposition are intricately linked.

If you are looking for a job and don't have an insider's view of what your target audience needs, do your homework. Ask friends in that field. Do a Google search on the company. Look them up in Yahoo Finance. Business analyst reports are a great way to see where companies' weak spots are. Go to LinkedIn and look at the backgrounds of the targets with whom you might be interviewing. Where might they be feeling insecure? For instance, say you are interviewing with a VP of Marketing who has spent most of his career on the technical and sales side and may feel inadequate as a marketer. You can position yourself as a strong career marketer who empowers teams with marketing skills transfer.

Never underestimate the importance of this step. How can you begin to position yourself as the answer to someone's problem if you aren't clear on who that person is and what the person's problems are?
Ask yourself: what kind of cake is your audience hungry for?

Value Proposition: How can *you* provide the solution?

Now, only after a thorough review of your audience and its needs, is the time to think about you. What do you have to offer *in relation to your audience's needs?* How can you be a real part of the solution? Perhaps you can add some muscle to their weakest parts and make *them* look like heroes. This is your value proposition.

An innovative American company was acquired by a large conservative European firm with a more formal corporate culture and less diverse workforce. The executives of the San Francisco company were concerned that with recent leadership changes, management looked less diverse, especially in the area of engineering. Celia, a process engineer, was able to differentiate herself by adding diversity leader to her positioning and leveraging her role as president of a national organization of female engineers. She became an asset to the executive team as they looked to raise the visibility of the company as an inclusive employer.

When applying for a job, *every* applicant will say he or she is a skilled programmer, accountant, manager—or whatever the title may be. That is a given. But what is your cake that adds differentiating value?

If you are interviewing with a company that is light on experience, and you've got a lot, emphasize your lengthy track record. If the opposite is true, emphasize your fresh perspective.

How can you help them reduce burdensome costs? Boost lagging sales? Change their culture? Find a pain point that your particular audience has today, and show how you can be—or at least be an important part of—the cure.

Differentiation: Why are you the best one to provide it?

You not only need to sell your solution to your target audience's problem, but you need to set yourself apart as *the* best person to deliver that solution. Start with your expertise. If you don't have it, get it. Take classes, read, engage with experts, do pro bono work.

Share your knowledge and be known for something of value.

Jeremy is a manager of data collection and metrics for a large software company. He is concerned about losing his job and wants to go from expendable to irreplaceable. He has assets that can help to distinguish himself but has not communicated them effectively. Jeremy has an MBA degree and marries business understanding with his technical understanding from his information technology background. This combined background enables him to provide the data that answers Marketing's strategic questions about campaigns. He needs to leverage his data collection systems expertise with his unique methodology for ensuring the right data is collected. By doing so, he will move his positioning from being a cog in a wheel to a key employee who adds strategic value.

Evidence: How can you prove it?

Here is where you show that you're not all talk. Find examples. Look back through your professional experience, and see what relates to what you are promising. What you've done in the past can translate into evidence of how you can deliver solutions. This can require some creative thinking—and looking at your experience in a new way. What you've done in one area can translate into meaningful proof of what you can deliver in another.

Marnie wanted to transition from a 20-year career in retail fashion sales to getting a job in the elder care industry, a move that would satisfy her soul. How could she be a credible job candidate when she hadn't done any professional work in the industry in decades? What was her evidence?

Her initial goal was a sales job with companies providing home care for seniors. To show her interest in elder care, she volunteered as a pet therapist with Alzheimer's patients, joined elder care networking groups and worked as a caregiver for an elderly patient. For evidence of her sales and service capability, she highlighted her Customer Service All-Star award for a leading retailer and promoted her excellent sales record of achievement. Finally, she demonstrated professional knowledge by talking about her early career experience as a social worker for elder care facilities and her college degrees in psychology and counseling. Her caring nature came through as she discussed how she had taken care of her mother, a longtime Parkinson's patient, in her mom's final years.

We helped Marnie to differentiate herself and package her assets in a way that spoke to the needs of her target audience, overcoming whatever prejudices they might have had about her long career in retail fashion sales. The result? Marnie got multiple interviews, and is working in elder care sales with a leading home care company.

To use the famous rubber-band analogy, create your goals far enough above what you are doing now to keep the rubber band taut. If it's slack, your aspirations may be too low—you may not be growing as you should. But don't set your sights so far away from your present reality that the rubber band breaks. Likewise, it's okay to stretch how skills in one area can apply to evidence in another. Just don't break the rubber band. If you stretch too much, you won't be credible.

> **You can't develop a sustainable new personal brand based on smoke and mirrors.**

If you are light on evidence, you now know where to start. What can you do here and now—from your current position, or lack of one—to show you can deliver solutions to your target audience? If you want to be known as an innovator, what are you doing now as proof that is the case? Don't have the opportunity to show that potential where you are now? Think outside the cubicle. Volunteer. Teach. Get involved in community groups where you can bring out the characteristics you want to shine. These quickly become evidence of what you can offer in a professional context.

Sample Positioning Statements

Let's look at a number of positioning charts and positioning statements to see how they can work in tandem.

Figure 2.4

Celia, Manager of Business Process Engineering
Goal: Promotion as Business Process Engineering Executive

Target Audience	For the VP Operations and Executive Management Team
Problem Statement	Who need to streamline processes and reduce costs to keep competitive, and are concerned about a lack of diversity in engineering
Category	I am a business process engineering manager and diversity leader who solves complex business problems.
Value Proposition	I have saved millions of dollars through streamlining business processes and have raised our company's image among women engineers.
Competitive Differentiation	Unlike other business process engineering managers, I am the president of a national organization for women engineers, and have recruited and built a diverse high-performing team that has delivered nearly 30 operational cost-cutting initiatives.

Chart Your Position

I recommend charting your specialty and key differentiator on a two-by-two matrix to see if you can find the right combination to give you a positioning advantage over your competitors. Put your specialty on the vertical y *axis* and put your key differentiation on the horizontal x *axis*. Who are your competitors? They might be fellow job seekers, other entrepreneurs seeking funding or those who are in line for the promotion you want. Your goal is to position yourself in the upper right-hand quadrant—the most advantaged position.

Here is Celia's positioning in a visualization.

Figure 2.5
Positioning Chart

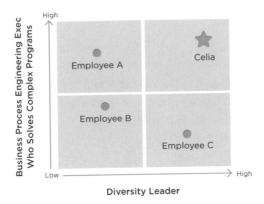

By adding Diversity Leader to her positioning chart, Celia is differentiating herself from other business process engineering experts in the company. Look for areas that help to set you apart but that you may currently discount. Take a fresh look at everything you have done or could do, then brainstorm how this expertise or experience could be of value to your company given current trends and pain points. You may surprise yourself with a unique way of differentiating your value.

Figure 2.6
Marcus, Software Engineer

Goal: Promotion and recognition in existing company, or new job opportunity

Target Audience	For the CEO and Executive Team at software companies
Problem Statement	Who need to grow the business with new products but are concerned about the innovation pipeline and engineering talent management
Category	I am a product engineering executive and innovation expert
Value Proposition	Who builds a culture of innovation that decreases development time and results in products that wow customers.

Competitive Differentiation	Unlike other product development executives, I have developed proven management techniques for innovation culture change and have a track record of recruiting and retaining high-performing engineers.

Marcus's original positioning as a VP of Engineering with no other clarification does not differentiate him among other engineering executives. By adding "innovation expert" and talking about his innovation culture techniques and engineering talent management track record, he rises above the crowd and presents a compelling story. He is now positioned as a technologist skilled in human resources and culture—a rare combination.

If you seem to be a plain-vanilla manager, find some area or management practice in which you can excel. For example, can you be expert in a domain or skill area, a geographic area, a management technique or attribute, or an area of thought leadership? You may be able to leverage some capability or training from your past that just needs dusting off and repackaging. I had a client who had spent so many years in marketing that she forgot she had a degree in biology. By calling attention to her science education, we were able to position her credibly for a new job opportunity partnering with the company's top scientists.

Figure 2.7

Asha, Entrepreneurial CEO

Goal: Get VC funding for start-up

Target Audience	For venture capitalists funding cloud-based software startups
Problem Statement	Who want to participate in the market for Big Data analytics based in the cloud
Category	I am the technology founder and CEO of a scalable, cloud-based service for Big Data analytics and visualizations for business
Value Proposition	Who has the startup track record, technology vision and management background to become the cloud-based leader in Big Data.

Competitive Differentiation	Unlike other Big Data entrepreneurs, I have a proven track record of selling a technology vision, scaling operations and building global teams to meet the demands of business customers.

Asha's original positioning was solely as a CEO for a data analytics company. By adding the terms "cloud-based service," "Big Data" and "visualizations," she hit upon three keywords that made her and her company more interesting given current trends. In addition to being a technologist, she is positioning herself as an experienced start-up CEO who can sell a vision, scale and build a global company—all music to the ears of potential investors. She is painting a picture of how the company will be successful in marketing *and* operations.

Figure 2.8
Lee, Recent MBA Graduate
Goal: Find first job with new MBA degree

Target Audience	For hiring managers at global management consulting firms
Problem Statement	Who want to expand in new markets with recent MBAs who can come up to speed quickly on technology, global markets and client consulting
Category	I am an MBA-trained business strategist and software project leader with Chinese language fluency and market understanding.
Value Proposition	I can provide immediate value to a wide range of client teams through my domain knowledge and capabilities in research, strategy development and project management.
Competitive Differentiation	Unlike other recent MBA graduates, I'm a software engineering leader who has led deadline-oriented project teams, and lived and traveled in Asia. I speak Mandarin and Cantonese (in addition to my native English).

Lee's key differentiation is combining software engineering leadership, his MBA training and his global experience and language capabilities. His ability to "provide immediate value" speaks to the needs of management consulting firms who need to get new consultants productive quickly. You may not have Lee's résumé upon graduation from business school, but you can still market capabilities that employers seek. For instance, you can show project management experience through leading teams in your MBA program or doing something similar on a volunteer basis for an outside organization.

Figure 2.9

Mike, Software Engineer

Goal: Recognition as Visionary in Open Source Software

Target Audience	For the CTO and Executive Team
Problem Statement	Who require industry-wide adoption of our technology to realize the corporate vision
Category	I am an open source software visionary with a proven track record of industry leadership and execution
Value Proposition	Who can accelerate industry adoption and standardization around our technology.
Competitive Differentiation	Unlike other open source developers, I can deliver technology initiatives and drive open source projects that further corporate objectives.

We met Mike at the beginning of this chapter as a programmer who strategically positioned himself in new technology areas, that is, graphical web software. The positioning statement above shows how he is shifting his focus to open-source software and differentiating himself as a visionary leader who can execute.

Iterate to Hone Your Positioning

Iteration is key to making your positioning statement crisp and compelling. If you change the target audience, the problem statement changes and, hence, the value proposition. Conversely, you may have a great value proposition but if it doesn't match the audience's needs, you need to find a new target audience that will value what you have to offer.

> **The key to great positioning is putting yourself in the shoes of the audience that you are trying to reach.**

For product companies, the key is understanding the consumer. For those looking for a job, it is understanding the needs of the hiring manager. For the entrepreneur looking for funding, it is understanding the needs of investors. If you have a skill that is unique to you but no one is interested, it doesn't matter that it is unique. You have to be *relevant* and unique.

Chapter 2 Summary

- Positioning provides the rational foundation (cake) for branding. Positioning makes your brand credible.

- Positioning articulates your unique value and provides meaningful differentiation.

Chapter 2 Action List

- ○ Understand your goal and use the triangulation model to determine what your best positioning strategy is to achieve your goal.

- ○ Fill out the positioning statement for your most important audience.

- ○ Then, fill out the positioning statement again with a different audience. Note how the problem statement and value proposition change. See chapter 3 (Figure 3.6) for a template to develop value messages by audience.

- ○ Visualize your positioning in a positioning chart (see Celia's example in Figure 2.5) and place your competitors in the different quadrants. If the upper right-hand quadrant is crowded, you need to find positioning elements that will better differentiate you.

Messaging

Step 2: Messaging

Message for Clarity and Impact

Sam is an independent consultant who goes to a lot of networking events to drum up new business. He's a personable guy who has no trouble approaching a stranger and starting a conversation. He will chat for a few minutes, exchange business cards, then move on to someone new.

The trouble is that he can't define what he does in a clear and memorable way. Sam is a consultant who wants to be all things to all people. He says he does market research, market segmentation strategies, pricing, sales training and copywriting. After people meet him, they don't remember what he does or why they should ever call him.

When you meet people for the first time, they will remember only one or two things about who you are. What do you want to leave them with?

Contrast Sam's example with an experience with my dentist, who started my latest exam with "I know you are the branding expert, and I wanted to know . . ." When your dentist nails your positioning, you know that you are doing a good job of brand messaging.

The root of Sam's messaging problem is that his positioning category is not clear. Is he a marketing consultant, a pricing specialist, a sales trainer or a copywriter? If you are not clear on your positioning strategy, go back to chapter 2, because without a clear category and differentiated value, you won't be able to develop compelling messages.

If you have a solid positioning strategy, you're ready to start on BrandingPays Step 2, which is where we develop the key messages that will be used in all of our verbal communications—both written and spoken.

The words you choose to describe yourself and what you offer are important. If the words are clear and compelling, they will resonate with your target audience. Your messages should articulate your positioning and provide evidence for the claims you make.

The Elevator Pitch and Your Evidence

Madeleine, a high-tech entrepreneur, was at a networking event where all participants were given 30 seconds to introduce themselves. She stood up and began to ramble about different scenarios where her product was needed. At the end of her 30 seconds, her audience couldn't remember what she or her company did. She missed an opportunity to brand herself and her company.

What Madeleine needed was an elevator pitch, a set of talking points that would help her to answer succinctly "What do you do?" or "Tell me about yourself."

Having a set of talking points will help you take advantage of an opportunity to position yourself—no matter where you are, even if it's between floors on an elevator ride.

A perfect example of using an elevator pitch to take advantage of an unexpected opportunity is Jenna. Recently, she spotted a CEO of a biotech company eating alone in her local restaurant. She had worked with him briefly at her current firm when he was a senior vice president there, but she wasn't sure he remembered her. Armed with an elevator pitch that she had prepared in advance, she confidently introduced herself. The CEO asked her to sit down and they chatted about her current company and the industry for 15 minutes. When she rose to leave, she told him that if he ever had need for a senior corporate lawyer with strong commercial experience, she would be interested. He had her sit down again, and after another discussion, nearly offered her a job on the spot. Within two weeks, she got her dream job as an executive with this company. Jenna's compelling elevator pitch helped her make a favorable impression that led to a great job offer.

See Figure 3.1 for a template for developing your elevator pitch.

Figure 3.1

Elevator Pitch

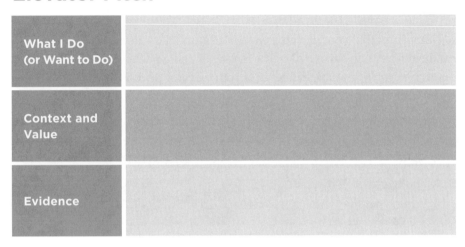

The elevator pitch template will help you to organize your talking points into three categories:

- What I Do (or Want to Do)
- Context and Value
- Evidence

The "What I Do" section should include keywords that your audience can remember after meeting you. For Hillary Freeman, the City Council candidate, the most important thing was for voters to remember her name and associate it with the City Council race. Often when I meet people, they launch into other subjects so quickly that I haven't caught their name and have no idea who they work for or what they do. Establish your name and what you do (or hope to do) up front.

The "Context and Value" section should help your audience understand the importance of what you do and how you are positioning yourself. The context for Hillary was shared values and bringing city policies and community values into balance. You need to establish what is happening in the world that makes your job and ability so compelling. If we don't think what you do is important, it's unlikely your audience will pay much attention to the rest of your elevator pitch.

The "Evidence" section should include proof points of the claims you are making.

Hillary, for example, backs up her claim of having the "right business skills and community values" with her business executive and community leadership experience.

It's important that your elevator pitch not sound like a canned speech, which can be off-putting. No one likes the feeling of being pitched by a salesperson. Try to find ways to weave elements of your elevator pitch into a conversation without sounding rehearsed or boastful.

Remember, the elevator pitch should be your talking points. Find creative ways of weaving them into conversations.

If you have limited time to give your elevator pitch, consider this guide:

5 seconds: Say your name and what you do (or want to do).

30 seconds: Add the context and your value messages.

60 seconds or beyond: Add examples of your evidence. You can include examples and metrics. You might weave in some stories that highlight the points you are trying to make.

The positioning statement should feed the messaging in your elevator pitch. See how Hillary's positioning statement and her elevator pitch are related in Figure 3.2 and Figure 3.3.

Figure 3.2

Sample Positioning Statement for Hillary

Target Audience	For Palo Alto voters
Problem Statement	Who feel that city policies and budget are not always aligned with neighborhood concerns and priorities, and are looking for new leadership that engages the community in solutions
Category	I am a high-tech business executive and community leader with the right mix of business management skills and community values to lead Palo Alto into the future
Value Proposition	Who will provide new leadership by listening to citizens and balancing community needs with fiscal realities.
Competitive Differentiation	I'm a business and community leader who shares your values, and am: • Not afraid to ask the hard questions • Committed to building community-based solutions • Experienced in the management of change and in fiscal accountability

Sample Elevator Pitches

Figure 3.3

Sample Elevator Pitch for Hillary

What I Do (or Want to Do)	I'm Hillary Freeman, and I'm running for City Council.
Context and Value	I love Palo Alto and want to bring our policies and our community values into balance. I'm a business and community leader who shares your values. I am: • Not afraid to ask the hard questions • Committed to building community-based solutions • Experienced in the management of change and in fiscal accountability
Evidence	I believe I have the right mix of business skills and community values to lead Palo Alto into the future. I share your values as a mother, wife of a business owner, and local leader on the YMCA board, PTA Council, Libraries Now! Committee, Children's Theater and youth sports. I'm also a software company executive who has experience in fiscal accountability, and business and change management.

Although Hillary kept her overarching messages the same (e.g., marriage of business skills and community values for new leadership), she tailored her evidence and examples according to her audience. For library lovers, she emphasized her founding membership in Libraries Now!, a grassroots group that worked to introduce a bond measure for improving libraries. For the school community, she stressed her PTA leadership, her role as a mother of schoolchildren and her volunteering in youth sports. Depending on your audience, you may have different elevator pitches.

Gloria, a procurement director at a large global company, told me that after completing our BrandingPays program, she found herself on the train with the newly appointed chief procurement officer (her manager's manager). The train ride was going to be over an hour long and she knew she should take the opportunity to position herself with him. At first, she panicked. What was she going to say? But then she remembered that she had developed an elevator pitch with a value proposition for executives, and decided to try it out. Her introduction to him went well, and they talked at length about her role at the company and her ideas for instituting global best practices. Her goal was to have this senior executive know who she was and to position herself as a strategic contributor. Gloria's elevator pitch helped her to come across as articulate and present her role in a strategic global context. Mission accomplished!

An elevator pitch will give you confidence to meet new people in any setting because you know you have talking points to use.

Figure 3.4 is an example of an elevator pitch that positions Gloria as a strategic thinker and leader with company executives.

Figure 3.4

Sample Elevator Pitch for Internal Networking with Executives

What I Do (or Want to Do)	I'm Gloria Jeffries, the director of global procurement.
Context and Value	Procurement has never been more important than in today's economic environment.
	To be globally competitive, we must streamline and consolidate purchasing with a balanced approach--one that assesses risks and options for global supply.
Evidence	We recently completed a global best practices study. We will soon be starting pilot programs at our company based on some interesting practices from leaders in other industries. From the standpoint of our own industry, we found that our company is the gold standard for best practices (*provide metrics*).

How do you use your elevator pitch at networking events? It's important to be yourself and to use your own words that sound natural. Remember that a conversation should not be an opportunity for you to talk nonstop about yourself. If someone asks you about yourself, say a few sentences to establish your positioning credibility, then ask the person about him- or herself. You will find opportunities throughout this give-and-take to weave in your key messages. Remember that your mission is education, not mere promotion. Ask yourself, "What is the one key thing that people will remember about me?" If they look at your business card after the event, will they remember that you are a purchasing exec or whatever you are, and connect with you later if they have a need in your area of expertise?

Figure 3.5

Sample Elevator Pitch for External Networking

What I Do (or Want to Do)	I'm George Paulsen of XYZ Law. I'm a lawyer who specializes in intellectual property.
Context and Value	Protecting intellectual property (IP) is key for companies whose fortunes rise and fall on their innovations.
Evidence	I recently helped a Fortune 500 company protect their IP interests when they spun off a technology business. I enjoy speaking to industry groups on the topic of managing the legal issues in innovation.

By setting the context for why protecting intellectual property is important to business, George will likely get asked follow-on questions probing what he means. At that point, he could bring up a recent project he worked on with a Fortune 500 company. This exchange of ideas will come across as a natural conversation and not as a sales pitch.

However, within a few sentences, George will have positioned himself as a credible IP lawyer. People who meet him will consider recommending him as a speaker to their industry group if innovation or IP are topics of interest.

Figure 3.6

Sample Elevator Pitch for MBA Graduate Looking for a Job

What I Do (or Want to Do)	I'm Lee Chang. I recently graduated from XYZ University with an MBA degree.
Context and Value	I'd like to find a job with a global management consulting firm. I think clients could benefit from my background in software engineering management, business analysis and strategy skills. Working with Chinese clients would be great since I know the culture and the language.
Evidence	I know that I'd fit into a fast-paced consulting environment because I've had to lead deadline-oriented development teams. In business school, my project team won the contest for best business plan.

Remember Lee's positioning example in chapter 2? This elevator pitch is an example of how he could message his positioning value.

Depending on how the conversation went, he could bring up different evidence points. The overall impression of Lee is positive because he comes across as someone who knows what he wants and how to get it. This is the type of personality that management consulting firms seek to hire.

Figure 3.7

Sample Elevator Pitch for External Networking

What I Do (or Want to Do)	I'm a product development executive for 123 Company with a passion for enhancing innovation in engineering cultures.
Context and Value	My mantra is "innovate or die." I've developed some unique practices for creating a more supportive and productive culture of innovation.
Evidence	The results have been outstanding. We are developing new technology products twice as fast as before. And, we are attracting and retaining excellent engineers because of the way we empower our development teams to innovate.

This product development executive is positioning herself as a leader in innovation with evidence that backs up her words. Whether you differentiate yourself in diversity, innovation or another domain, you can use this one-word or one-concept association as a sort of brand shorthand that people can remember.

How do you use your elevator pitch at networking events? It's important to be yourself and to use your own words that sound natural. Remember that a conversation should not be an opportunity for you to talk nonstop about yourself. A two-way conversation will engage others and will still afford you opportunities to weave in your key messages.

Different Value Messages for Different Audiences

If you are a professional manager, your value message to your staff or cross-functional partners will be different from your value message to the CEO. If you are an MBA graduate looking for a job, your value message to a management consulting firm will be different from your message to a manufacturing firm. If you are an entrepreneur, your value message to potential investors will be different from your value message to customers or job candidates.

The reasons for different value messages should be clear. Your audiences have different goals, different problems to solve—that is, different needs. The compelling reason to hire you or to do business with you will vary according to those needs.

The positioning statement can be used to develop different value messages. In addition, it is helpful to see how the messages differ by audience on one page. The Value Messages by Audience matrix will help you to understand the shifts in messaging at a glance.

Figure 3.8

Value Messages by Audience

	Audience 1	Audience 2	Audience 3
Audience Needs/Wants			
Audience Challenge			
Value Message			

Figure 3.9

Value Messages by Audience

Example for Marketing Director for Pharmaceutical Company

	Sales	CFO	CEO
Audience Needs/Wants	Meet sales targets	Grow revenues and margins in line with Wall Street expectations	Maintain integrity and value of corporate brand
Audience Challenge	Negative media about the high cost of therapeutic drug treatments	Concerned about high marketing expenses that reduce margins	Market concerns about losing innovative edge with merger
Value Message	Increased PR and education about the high cost of drug innovation. Developed messages for sales team to meet concerns re costs	Creative brand marketing that reduces traditional marketing expenses while supporting brand growth	Brand marketing and industry thought leadership underscore innovation and being patient-driven (company brand value)

Back Your Positioning Claims with Evidence Messages

In your positioning statement, you are making certain claims that need to be backed up by proof points in order to be credible. Your proof points will be put into your evidence messages. Sometimes it is helpful to organize these messages into buckets so they will be at your fingertips.

Let's look at how Celia might evidence her positioning as a processing engineering manager and diversity leader who is a complex problem solver.

Positioning Claim

Business Process Engineering Manager and Diversity Leader

Evidence

Business Process Engineering Manager and Expertise

- Built high-performing team that delivered breakthrough results in business process management (with success metrics)

- Six Sigma Black Belt

- B.S. and M.S. degrees in Engineering

- National engineering awards

- Publications

Complex Problem Solver

- Instrumental in streamlining operations as leader of nearly 30 operational cost-cutting initiatives that delivered millions of dollars in Net Present Value and cost avoidance

- Overhauled complex IT portfolio management processes and documented achievements through an engineering scorecard

- Led cross-functional and multi-geographic teams in Six Sigma methodology, saving tens of millions of dollars

Diversity Leader

- Demonstrated diverse hiring in my teams

- President of national women's engineering organization

- Worked with executive management on strategies to position the company as an attractive employer for women engineers

How the Positioning Statement Can Feed Your LinkedIn Profile

LinkedIn has become one of the world's most important professional networks, and it is where many recruiters and hiring managers go to find candidates. Others will often look up your profile before meeting with you, so your LinkedIn profile may set the first impression.

The positioning work in the BrandingPays System provides the basis for developing a LinkedIn profile that will set you apart in a positive way.

We'll use Celia again as an example. How can Celia translate her positioning work into compelling copy for her LinkedIn profile?

I always encourage professionals to write a headline and summary in LinkedIn before the chronological detail to position themselves for job or business opportunities. Here's a sample LinkedIn profile for Celia.

Business Process Engineering Executive and Diversity Leader

Solving complex problems and encouraging diversity hiring are two hallmarks of my leadership in business process engineering. A strong background in engineering gives me the analytical framework for simplifying complexity. As a business process engineering executive for XYZ Corporation, I built a high-performance team charged with reducing manufacturing costs. We developed 30 cost-cutting initiatives that resulted in millions of dollars in cost-savings through streamlined operations.

I also enjoy being a role model for women in technology leadership. While serving as the president of a national organization for female engineers, I worked with our executive leadership to bring recognition of XYZ Corp. as a good place for women in technology.

In two short paragraphs, Celia was able to communicate her positioning in business processing engineering and diversity leadership, as well as provide some high-level evidence backing up her positioning claims. She comes across as a confident, capable leader who is differentiated by her engineering background, complex problem-solving skills and diversity leadership. The fact that her profile is well written speaks to her communication skills.

Your LinkedIn profile can be written in the first person (I) or third person (he or she), depending on which voice serves your story better. Although some branding experts suggest injecting your personality into your profile, my advice is to err on the side of being conservative and businesslike. A profile that raises eyebrows may damage rather than promote your chances of getting a job or a new business opportunity. A telephone call or in-person meeting provides a better channel to convey your personality.

Avoid too many superlatives in your messaging. They can detract rather than add to your credibility. It is best to demonstrate your superior skills or value through evidence messages.

What Is Your Tagline?

Writing a sample tagline is one of the best exercises you can do to make crystal clear what your positioning category is. For the purpose of this exercise, we will focus on your cake or rational value, which is the most important thing for a prospective employer or investor to understand. Examples of taglines: an engineer who is the "Open Source Software Visionary" or a corporate lawyer who is the "Strategic IP Expert." Your tagline could be your headline for your LinkedIn profile summary.

Chapter 3 Summary

- An elevator pitch is a set of talking points to help you articulate your positioning in a clear and concise way.

Chapter 3 Action List

- o　Write your elevator pitch.

- o　Back up your positioning claims by listing your proof points as evidence messages.

- o　Write your LinkedIn profile and have someone you trust edit it for you.

Brand Strategy

Step 3: Brand Strategy

How to Develop Your Brand Strategy

Hillary Freeman, the city council candidate, was the poster child for branding from the inside out. Her inner passion, creative ideas and desire to engage were reflected in how she communicated her brand externally. She *was* the new face of Palo Alto leadership, from her ideas and her website to how she dressed and connected with others.

Whether you are a professional looking for a job or career change or an entrepreneur looking for funding, you need a brand strategy that puts your cake and icing together for maximum results. A good brand strategy will help guide you in everything you need to do to speed achievement of your goal. When you brand consistently, you help the world know what to think and say about you.

Hillary brought her cake and icing together in a Brand Strategy Platform, a tool that helped to ensure that all brand communications from the candidate's behavior to the campaign's marketing programs were in sync with the strategy. We'll explain the Brand Strategy Platform later in this chapter, but first let's look at a simpler view.

Figure 4.1 shows a simplified view of Hillary's cake (rational value) and icing (emotional value). The cake goal is written at the top. In the table below are two examples of icing: one that does not support her cake and one that does. By the way, Hillary's real icing did, in fact, support her cake. We've included the contrasting column to illustrate what kind of icing would not have supported Hillary's brand.

Figure 4.1

Hillary's Cake (Rational Brand Value)

New face of leadership—a business leader who shares our community values (with ideas, passion and engagement)

ICING does not support CAKE	ICING supports CAKE
Boring, old-fashioned style	Professional yet fresh visual style
Uninspiring web presence	Unique website that looks contemporary and engages
Low energy, lack of passion	High-energy, passionate about ideas
Keeps to self, avoids engagement	Reaches out and connects with empathy
Frown or pursed-lip smile	Genuine, wide smile

How do you marry cake and icing in your brand? Our brand strategy platform (Figure 4.2) provides the answer. The platform is a 360-degree view of your brand that will help you to deliver on that brand in thought, word and deed. Don't worry if you feel that this template looks daunting; we'll take it a section at a time to make it easier to use. This one-page brand strategy platform will encourage you to boil your thoughts down to their essence—the key to good branding. You will use this template twice—first, to capture your current brand and second, to map out your desired brand.

Figure 4.2

Brand Strategy Platform

Core Values	Strengths (Cake)	Personality (Icing)	Brand Image (Cake & Icing)	Brand Promise (Cake & Icing)
1. 2. 3. 4.	Hard Skills	Personality Attributes	Brand Associations	Rational Value
What I love doing	Soft Skills	Type of leader, working, friend	External Image	Emotional Value
My life/career dreams Short-term: Long-term:	Expertise	Brand Metaphor	Relationship Image	Brand Experience

The brand strategy platform represents our methodology in template form. Think of it as a worksheet to help you to understand who you are and what your brand stands for. The brand strategy platform augments the positioning statement (chapter 2) by incorporating your icing. Few people think strategically about the emotional value that their brand delivers, and fewer still can articulate what it is. The brand strategy platform provides the vehicle to help you to put into words the essence and value of your brand.

Let's take a section-by-section look at the brand strategy platform to help you understand how to use it. I'll use Hillary Freeman as an example throughout each section to model how it is done. Other examples of brand strategy platforms will be included at the end of this chapter.

Core Values (Cake and Icing)

Core values should drive the behaviors you engage in and the decisions that you make.

> **When you align your brand execution with your core values, your brand will be more authentic and credible.**

We've added areas to help you explore what you love doing and your dreams in career and life—both goals that should be driven by core values. You may be surprised by what you discover when filling out the core values column.

Figure 4.3

Core Values
1. Transparency
2. Passion
3. Engagement

What I love doing

Making a difference through creative ideas and engagement

My life/ career dreams

Short-Term: Become a City Council member
Long-Term: Become a motivational speaker

Core Values Box (top): Core Values

What are the core values that drive who you are and what you are all about? Core values help you to have meaning in what you do and to "do the right thing" in your business, career, relationships and life. Try to narrow the list to just a handful of items. For instance, *trust, transparency, honesty* and *integrity* express similar values, so in the interest of brevity, pick one of these rather than including all of them. If necessary, you can develop a backup document that expounds on what you mean by that one word.

Hillary's Core Values:

- Transparency
- Passion
- Engagement

Hillary's core values were true to her person as well as being meaningful to the electorate, which was hungry for passionate leaders who engaged well with the public in an open and democratic process.

Core Values Box (middle): What I Love Doing

Figuring out what you love doing is important. If you love doing a certain job or activity, then you'll have a passion for it. You'll have more energy and creativity—you'll do your best work. Your passion and enthusiasm will come across in your personality, making you more attractive and engaging.

Sometimes when filling out this box, there can be a big "Aha!" moment when you discover that what you love doing and what you are currently doing are not in sync. This one section caused a personal branding client of mine to move from marketing to a lateral job in another area that better leveraged her interest and degree in science.

It is not always practical to drop your career and become, for example, a jazz musician. Perhaps you can find some of the things that you love about jazz (such as improvisation, creativity and teamwork) and find opportunities to do more of this in your current job or in an adjacent career path.

What Hillary Loves Doing:
Making a difference through creative ideas and engagement

It's clear that her goal of becoming a City Council member aligns with her love of making a difference by leveraging creative thought and engaging with the public. Does your job or career align with what you love doing?

Core Values Box (bottom): My Life or Career Dreams

Few of us take the time to think about what we want out of our lives or our careers. Here's your chance. Envision yourself engaged in what you'd like to be doing in 10 or 20 years. Then, imagine looking back and seeing what steps or paths you took to get there.

Try writing down a short-term career goal, and then a longer-term career or life goal. You can develop a brand strategy for today's career goal, but keep your longer-term goal in mind as your brand changes throughout the years.

Hillary's Life or Career Dreams:
- Short-term: Become a City Council member
- Long-term: Become a motivational speaker who inspires us to create a better world

Figure 4.4

Strengths (Cake)
Hard Skills --Business analytics --Budgeting --Auditing --Sales
Soft Skills --Management --Public speaking --Team building and collaboration --Networking --Creative problem solving
Expertise/Experience --Sales and marketing executive --Palo Alto Schools, Site Council President & PTA --YMCA Board Member --Children's Theatre Board Member --Youth sports coach & referee --Libraries Now! Founding Member --BA Marine Biology, MS Fisheries Biology

Hillary has since left the world of high-tech sales to follow her passion for making a difference with young people. She leveraged her science degrees to become a middle-school science teacher and a Google Education Fellow. She has expanded the horizons of her students with educational trips to China, Japan, Spain and Trinidad. Hillary has co-authored a book on conflict resolution that brands her as an expert. She is a speaker and trainer at national conferences. Clearly, she is setting the foundation to realize her long-term goal.

Strengths (Cake)

The Strengths section helps you to articulate both the hard and soft skills as well as the expertise that make up your strengths. The Strengths column represents your cake, or rational value. Look at your positioning statement (chapter 2) to understand the strengths that should evidence your positioning claim.

As you inventory your strengths, also identify key weaknesses that may hinder your progress toward your desired brand. These weaknesses can be addressed in your action plan (chapter 6). We have chosen not to include a box for weaknesses, as our focus is on keeping this exercise positive.

Strengths Box (top): Hard Skills

Hard skills are something you were specifically trained to do, such as software programming, speaking a foreign language, market research or financial analysis. Hard skills use your Intelligence Quotient (IQ).

Hillary's Hard Skills:

- Business analytics
- Budgeting
- Auditing
- Sales

Hillary's hard skills helped her to be credible when she campaigned as a candidate with business experience who knew how to budget, analyze and conduct audits.

Are the skills required for you to achieve your career or business goals in your Strengths column? If not, then add them to Strengths in your desired brand with an asterisk for action (we'll address building needed skills in your action plan in chapter 6).

Strengths Box (middle): Soft Skills

Soft skills can be thought of as people skills. Don't get hung up on what are hard skills versus soft skills. The important thing is to list all of your strength attributes—both the obvious and the less obvious, or less tangible. You can edit the list later.

Soft skills rely more on your Emotional Quotient (EQ). Soft skills can include such skills as communicating, conflict management, human relations, making presentations, negotiating, team building, leadership skills, management skills, networking, collaboration and demonstrating empathy.

Hillary's Soft Skills:

- Management
- Public speaking
- Team building and collaboration
- Networking
- Creative problem solving

All of Hillary's soft skills were necessary to be an effective member of the City Council. She was able to message and demonstrate all of them through campaign events and her volunteer activities.

Strengths Box (bottom): Expertise and Experience

In the professional world, being an expert in a domain area is important. Generalists without special skills, knowledge or experience are often seen as commodities that are expendable. If you don't have an area of expertise, it is important to develop one. For instance, it can be a technical area, a market area or an area in which you provide thought leadership, such as managing diversity.

Maybe you need to dust off an old educational degree to show evidence of your expertise. Remember Marnie from chapter 2? She is the retail professional turned elder care sales specialist who emphasized her psychology and counseling degrees to build credibility for her career change.

Hillary's Expertise and Experience:

- Sales and Marketing executive
- Palo Alto Schools, Site Council president and PTA
- YMCA, board member
- Children's Theatre, board member
- Youth sports coach and referee
- Libraries Now! founding member
- BA Marine Biology, MS Fisheries Biology

Hillary had an excellent background in business and community, providing evidence for her brand positioning.

Personality (Icing)

The Personality column is all about icing, your emotional value or how people connect with you. For some technical jobs where the focus is heavily on your cake, or rational value, personality may be less important. But if you are personable, you will always have a leg up over someone with little personality or a negative personality.

The Personality column should be about likability. When was the last time you went the extra mile to help someone you did not like? Exactly. Do people think of you as someone who they would want to lead their team, go out for drinks with or work on their project? What are those attributes that attract people to you and make them like you? When people like you, they feel an emotional connection. They will be more willing to help you or advocate for you.

You don't have to be an extrovert to have personality attributes that people admire and find attractive.

I know people who exude a calm confidence and empathy that make their quiet personalities desirable.

Some of your core values or soft skills (from your Strengths section) may also appear in your Personality column, such as being collaborative, honest and empathetic. It makes sense for certain values or EQ attributes to appear as a theme in several columns. That just means that these attributes are a strong part of your brand that you evidence in many ways.

Figure 4.5

Personality (Icing)
Personality Attributes --Passionate about ideas --Engaging --Friendly --Empathetic
Type of leader, worker, friend --Inclusive & inspiring leader --Hard worker --Trusted friend
Brand Metaphor Community Gardens. These colorful gardens, planted and maintained by residents, are a metaphor for Hillary's passion, engagement and community values as well as her fresh point of view and bright style.

Personality (top box): Personality Attributes

Personalities come in all flavors: passionate, cerebral, hard-edged, quiet, extroverted, witty or dull (hopefully, you are not the latter). Refer back to your goal. What kind of personality is more likely to achieve this goal? If you are looking for your first job and you lack confidence, companies won't want to hire you. If you are a sales manager and act like a loner, you will be less likely to reach your goal of sales executive, someone who needs to build and inspire a team. If you are an entrepreneur without passion for your ideas, you will be less likely to inspire someone to invest in your company or buy your products.

Having a positive personality matters.

Hillary's Personality Attributes:

- Passionate about ideas
- Engaging
- Friendly
- Empathetic

Hillary's personality is perfectly aligned with her core values, strengths (soft skills) and positioning.

Personality (middle box): Type of leader, worker, friend

The focus here is how you show up as a leader, a worker or a friend in terms of personality. Are you inspiring, supportive, trustworthy, direct and caring? Some of your answers may be included as soft skills under Strengths, but repeating them here is fine. If you want to be an executive, you'll want to focus on your leadership personality. If you are an individual contributor, your focus should be both on your worker and leadership personality, since all professionals should have leadership attributes.

Hillary's Type of Leader, Worker and Friend:

- Inclusive and inspiring leader
- Hard worker
- Trusted friend

We would not expect anything less of the Hillary Freeman brand, given what we know about her core values and how she is positioned.

Personality (bottom box): Brand Metaphor (Cake and Icing)

The brand metaphor can help to free you in how you think about your brand. For instance, finding a celebrity, retail store or car brand that personifies your brand can help you to be clear about your brand type. If a luxury hotel is your brand metaphor, you'll know that the highest-quality service and customer experience is key to what you are about. Your behaviors and communication should reflect these values.

Be creative when thinking about your brand metaphor. You can use any animate or inanimate thing as your metaphor. People have chosen kitchen appliances, museums, points of interest, animals and fashion brands. You can make it fun by polling your friends or colleagues about what metaphor they would use to represent your brand.

At the time, we didn't have a brand metaphor for Hillary, but if I had to choose one today, I would say:

> Community Gardens. These colorful gardens, planted and maintained by residents, are a metaphor for Hillary's passion for engagement and community values as well as her fresh point of view and bright style.

Figure 4.6

Brand Image (Cake and Icing)

The Brand Image section includes your brand associations, visual branding and relationship branding.

Articulating your brand image will help to keep you on track as you implement your brand in your communications, your wardrobe and how you relate to others.

Brand Image (top box): Brand Associations

You want people to associate you with your profession and unique positioning. Your branding has failed if all they remember is how you dress, not what you do or what value you provide.

For this template, focus your brand associations primarily on your cake, or positioning (see your positioning statement in chapter 2). Include bullet points for your positioning category and differentiating value. You'll have plenty of opportunity in the next boxes to add the icing.

Hillary Brand Associations:

• New face of leadership: Business leader with community values

• Passion and engagement

• Schools, libraries and youth sports advocate

These are the brand associations that we wanted associated with Hillary the candidate.

Brand Image (middle box): External Image

Your external image should include what you look like, your presence and your visual branding.

Hillary's External Image:

- Confident
- Fresh style and bright colors (logo and all visual branding)
- Professional but inviting look, including wardrobe
- Engaging website and brochure with contemporary design

Hillary's strategy for her external image reinforced her positioning messages about being the new face of leadership. Think about what messages your external image sends. If these messages are not consistent with your goal, consider changing your external brand strategy.

Brand Image (bottom box): Relationship Image

Are you seen as a supportive manager, a good partner and a trusted friend? How you treat others in a relationship demonstrates your values.

Hillary's Relationship Image:

- Warmth and humanity
- Supportive
- Trusting
- Respect for diversity

Hillary's ability to build warm, genuine relationships was an important part of her brand. She was a welcome contrast to many of the council candidates who had a more difficult time developing authentic and engaging relationships. She was definitely someone whom you would enjoy having coffee with and getting to know.

Figure 4.7

Brand Promise (Cake and Icing)

Brand Promise (Cake & Icing)
Rational Value New leadership that can solve Palo Alto problems by marrying business experience with community values
Emotional Value She makes me feel: --Heard & respected --I have a voice in government --Optimistic about the future
Brand Experience A passionate new leader marrying business know-how with community values who can solve our problems with citizen engagement

Core values, strengths, personality and brand image should deliver on your brand promise. When people choose your brand, they should get what has been advertised. To deliver anything less breaks your brand promise to your customer or target audience.

Brand Promise (top box): Rational Value

Rational value consists of what others should expect from your cake—that is, your functional value.

Hillary's Rational Brand Value:
New leadership that can solve Palo Alto problems by marrying business experience with community values

In Hillary's brand strategy platform, the recurring themes of new leadership and marrying business and community experience are woven throughout. Don't be afraid to sound like a broken record in your platform; if you see words or themes repeated, it means you are in alignment on many levels.

Brand Promise (middle box): Emotional Value

Emotional value is how people should feel when they engage with your brand. Using "I feel..." statements from your stakeholders' viewpoint can help you to understand what emotional value they might feel in working with you or relating to you. Do they feel relief, empowerment, secure that things will be done well, enjoyment or respect?

Hillary's Emotional Brand Value:
She makes me feel:

- Heard and respected

- I have a voice in government

- Optimistic about the future

Having an emotional connection is key. This connection is what breeds brand loyalty. Does drinking coffee with friends at Starbucks, for instance, make you feel warm and cozy? This emotional association with the brand makes you want to return. For Hillary, making people feel heard and optimistic was key to her emotional brand value.

Brand Promise (bottom box): Brand Experience

The brand experience is the overall experience that we want to deliver when others come into contact with our brand. The brand experience must deliver on your overall brand promise—both the rational value and the emotional value. Try to crystallize the experience in a short phrase that teams the essence of your cake (positioning) with key icing deliverables.

Hillary's Brand Experience:
A passionate new leader marrying business know-how with community values who can solve our problems with citizen engagement.

Hillary's brand experience goal meant that she had to:

- Speak passionately for her ideas in candidate forums and one-on-one with voters

- Consistently communicate how she would address Palo Alto problems using her business knowledge and community experience

- Engage citizens individually and in public campaign events

Hillary had the right core values and strategy to drive her behavior and campaign actions to deliver on this brand experience. With the right brand strategy and consistently delivering on her brand experience, Hillary went from political unknown to the top vote-getter in her election.

Figure 4.8

Hillary Freeman Brand Strategy Platform

Core Values	Strengths (Cake)	Personality (Icing)	Brand Image (Cake & Icing)	Brand Promise (Cake & Icing)
1. Transparency 2. Passion 3. Engagement	*Hard Skills* --Business analytics --Budgeting --Auditing --Sales	*Personality Attributes* --Passionate about ideas --Engaging --Friendly --Empathetic	*Brand Associations* --New face of leadership: business leader with community values --Passion & engagement --Schools, libraries & youth sports advocate	*Rational Value* New leadership that can solve Palo Alto problems by marrying business experience with community values
What I love doing Making a difference through creative ideas and engagement	*Soft Skills* --Management --Public speaking --Team building and collaboration --Networking --Creative problem solving	*Type of leader, worker, friend* --Inclusive & inspiring leader --Hard worker --Trusted friend	*External Image* --Confident --Fresh style & bright colors --Professional but inviting look, including wardrobe --Engaging website & brochure with contemporary design	*Emotional Value* She makes me feel: --Heard & respected --I have a voice in government --Optimistic about the future
My life/ career dreams **Short-Term:** Become a City Council member **Long-Term:** Become a motivational speaker	*Expertise/Experience* --Sales and marketing executive --Palo Alto Schools, Site Council President & PTA --YMCA Board Member --Children's Theatre Board Member --Youth sports coach & referee --Libraries Now! Founding Member --BA Marine Biology, MS Fisheries Biology	*Brand Metaphor* Community Gardens. These colorful gardens, planted and maintained by residents, are a metaphor for Hillary's passion, engagement and community values as well as her fresh point of view and bright style.	*Relationship Image* --Warmth and humanity --Supportive --Trusting --Respect for diversity	*Brand Experience* A passionate new leader marrying business know-how with community values who can solve our problems with citizen engagement

Key Brand Descriptors

A completed brand strategy platform is a lot to comprehend. Using the template in Figure 4.9, boil your brand strategy down to three or four key brand descriptors. Without having to reference your entire brand strategy platform, your key brand descriptors will help you to align your behaviors and image with your brand. Refer to them daily to stay "on brand."

As you choose these few brand descriptors, imagine listening in on someone describing who you are and why you would make a good hire, partner or investment (in Hillary's case, a good City Council member).

Hillary's Key Brand Descriptors:

1. New face of leadership for Palo Alto

2. Marries business experience and community values

3. Warm, engaging and a breath of fresh air

As Hillary's example above demonstrates, key brand descriptors should include a combination of cake and icing.

1. CAKE: Your positioning category (see Brand Associations)

2. CAKE: Your differentiated value (see Rational Value)

3. ICING: Key points in brand image (see External Image, Relationship Image and Emotional Value)

Lead with your cake, because this is the foundation of your brand value. A general formula for key brand descriptors for professionals is ⅔ cake to ⅓ icing.

Figure 4.9

Your Key Brand Descriptors

The Importance of Icing

Sway, The Irresistible Pull of Irrational Behavior, is a provocative book that makes a powerful argument about how we often disregard logic and act irrationally based on our biases or emotions. The authors show how using "warm" versus "cold" as a descriptor in a bio of a substitute college instructor made all the difference in how students rated the teacher at the end of class. The half of the class that read the bio that said the teacher was "warm" described the teacher after class as "good natured, considerate of others, informal, sociable, popular, humorous, and humane."[1] The half of the class that read the bio that said the teacher was "cold" described him later as "self-centered, formal, unsociable, unpopular, irritable, humorless, and ruthless."[2]

As authors Ori Brafman and Rom Brafman put it:

> . . . a single word has the power to alter our whole perception of another person—and possibly sour the relationship before it even begins. When we hear a description of someone, no matter how brief, it inevitably shapes our experience of that person.[3]

What does this mean for personal branding?

We discussed how cake is your rational positioning or value and how icing is your emotional connection or irrational value. Therefore, if the arguments in *Sway* are true, then icing is extremely important to how people perceive us

1. Brafman, Ori, and Brafman, Rom, *Sway* (New York: Broadway Books, 2008), 75.
2. Ibid.
3. Ibid.

and may bias people against us in spite of the rational evidence of our value. Let's keep it simple and examine two brand descriptors, "warm" and "cold," and how they might be represented in brand images and behaviors.

Figure 4.10

The Importance of Icing

Brand Descriptor	Brand Image	Brand Behaviors	Sample Actions
Warm personality	Smiling face/photo, warm colors, softer wardrobe and style	Behaviors underscore positive outlook, friendliness, consideration, empathy, support, responsiveness, sense of humor, humanity, and social ease.	Ask how people are doing. Ask how you can help. Acknowledge people's contribution and thank others publicly. Tell amusing stories. Introduce people to each other. Support social causes. Smile.
Cold personality	Unsmiling or closed-mouth smile/photo, lack of warm color palette, harder-edged wardrobe and style	Behaviors underscore negative outlook, selfishness, judgment, formality, aloofness, lack of humor and humanity, lack of social graces and ease	Denigrate people. Criticize without constructive feedback. Keep to self at social events. Don't take time to acknowledge or thank others. Be "all business" all the time without empathy or interest in people's lives. Frown and knit eyebrows.

The chart represents a fairly stark contrast between personalities that are perceived as warm versus cold. I realize that some people may be labeled as "cold" or "aloof" when in actuality they are just extremely shy. Many of us are born shy. Believe it or not, I was shy when I was younger, but I took steps to get over my shyness by thrusting myself into activities that required that I be more outgoing such as being a cheerleader, an actor in school plays, a member of the speech squad and a singer in choir and select groups, and taking on leadership roles in various volunteer organizations. As an adult, there are myriad opportunities to be a leader, a presenter, a host, a networker—all of which will help to build your confidence in interacting with and influencing other people. Get over being shy and increase the warmth that your personality generates. You will be rewarded with a more likable and well-regarded brand. Remember, humans are irrational beings, so never underestimate the importance of icing.

Sample Brand Strategy Platforms

Sample Brand Strategy Platform for a Systems Engineer
Goal: Lead enterprise-wide change management project

Figure 4.11
Desired Brand for Systems Engineer

Core Values	Strengths (Cake)	Personality (Icing)	Brand Image (Cake & Icing)	Brand Promise (Cake & Icing)
1. Engagement 2. Leading edge 3. Reliability 4. Enjoying life, enjoying others	*Hard Skills* --SAP solutions --Strong technical and systems background --Ability to streamline processes	*Personality Attributes* --Engaging --Positive --Direct --Creative	*Brand Associations* --SAP solutions expert --Strong team leader --Fun to work with	*Rational Value* SAP solutions expertise and team leadership
What I love doing Partnering with others to realize a vision	*Soft Skills* --Communications --Creative problem solver --Team building	*Type of leader, worker, friend* --Reliable --Delivers on promises --Helpful --You know where you stand	*External Image* --Geek chic --Confident --Honest --Likeable --Good communicator	*Emotional Value* Others feel... --Secure that project will go as planned --Have fun working together
My life/ career dreams **Short-Term:** Leading an enterprise-wide change management project	*Expertise* --SAP certification --Large company installations	*Brand Metaphor* MINI Cooper car --Retro yet modern --Efficient --Fun design	*Relationship Image* --Willing partner --Win/win attitude	*Brand Experience* --Smooth, transparent process with expert --Fun --Collaborative

In this example, our systems engineer has developed a brand strategy that can best be summarized by these key brand descriptors:

1. SAP solutions expert (cake)

2. Strong team leader who delivers on promises (cake)

3. Likable, engaging, fun to work with (icing)

He could be known as solely an information technology resource, but he has positioned himself as an SAP solutions expert, which is more specific and answers a need of groups that require SAP systems development. He further stands out because technical people are not always strong team leaders who communicate well. Under Brand Experience, he has put an asterisk after "smooth, transparent process" because he needs to work on making the SAP development process more transparent to his inside clients. As he rebrands as the SAP solutions expert, it is likely that he will earn his opportunity to do an enterprise-wide change management project on the SAP platform.

Sample Brand Strategy Platform for a Health Care Executive
Goal: Move from position in marketing to patient access

Figure 4.12

Desired Brand for Health Care Executive

Core Values	Strengths (Cake)	Personality (Icing)	Brand Image (Cake & Icing)	Brand Promise (Cake & Icing)
1. Thought leadership 2. Accountability 3. Helping others	*Hard Skills* --Strategic marketing and planning --Market research and analysis	*Personality Attributes* --Dynamic and direct --Passionate --Personable with a sense of humor	*Brand Associations* --Patient access expert --Managed care marketing --Change management leader	*Rational Value* --Patient access thought leader --Managed care marketing strategist --Team performance
What I love doing Helping patients gain access to the therapies they need	*Soft Skills* --People management --Team leadership --Adaptability --Cross-functional networking	*Type of leader, worker, friend* --Leads by example --Accountability is key --Mentors well --Honest	*External Image* --Professional, but warm appearance --Confident --Connected --Social and likeable	*Emotional Value Others feel...* --Empowered by my leadership --Confident of results --Valued
My life/ career dreams Health care advocate who helps close the gap in health care disparities	*Expertise* --Patient access --Managed care marketing --Change management --Master's degree Health Services Administration	*Brand Metaphor* Ellen DeGeneres --Warm, witty, and smart --Comfortable in own skin	*Relationship Image* --Trusted partner --Willing to help --Puts others at ease	*Brand Experience* Patient access leader who builds and empowers teams to achieve results in a supportive environment

The key brand descriptors for Pamela, who we met in chapter 2, are:

1. Patient access expert
2. Managed care marketing strategist
3. Warm, empowering, supportive

After identifying her strategy, Pamela worked on being known as a patient access expert, upgraded to a more professional look and scheduled time to be more "social," so she could connect better with her staff and colleagues. She rewrote her résumé so that it communicated that she was a patient access expert, not only in the headline and summary, but also in the detailed proof points. Her brand focus and implementation helped executive management to recognize her value outside of marketing. She quickly achieved her goal of moving into a new executive role in patient access. The following is an example of what she might have included in her desired brand strategy.

Tips to Complete Your Brand Strategy Platform

Start by capturing a snapshot of your current brand in the Brand Strategy Template. You can start with your own perceptions. However, it is helpful to augment your self-view with objective input from 360 assessment data, informal talks with others about their perceptions, or having stakeholders fill out the Personal Branding Assessment Questionnaire in chapter 1.

Next, write your goal at the top of the Brand Strategy Platform. Fill out the template again with a desired brand that will help you to reach your career or business goal. Revisit your positioning statement to understand the needs of your target audience.

Use bullet points and keep your language brief when filling out this template. Less is more. For example, you will be able to remember three core values, but you might not remember six.

On your Desired Brand Platform, do a quick comparison of where you want to go versus where you are today. Asterisk the areas that need work. We'll address what to do about these gaps in your Action Plan (chapter 6).

Completing your Brand Strategy Platform may require that you think about yourself in a way that you have never done before. Some people fill out this template and realize that they are in the wrong job or career, while others realize that they are in the right job and feel reenergized about their commitment to it. Whatever your case, the Brand Strategy Platform will give you a holistic view of your brand that will make you think, and, one hopes, give you the confidence to take action.

Chapter 4 Summary

- The Brand Strategy Platform marries your cake (rational value) and your icing (emotional value).

- Key elements: core values, strengths, personality, brand image and brand promise.

- It helps you to deliver on your brand in thought, image, word and deed.

Chapter 4 Action List

o   Describe your current brand in the template.

o   Develop your desired brand in the template. Ensure that answers in all categories (core values, strengths, brand personality, brand image and brand promise) align to provide a consistent brand view.

o   Note the gaps between current brand and desired brand—or those areas you have asterisked in your desired brand. (How to improve your brand will be addressed in the Action Plan in chapter 6.)

o   On a separate sheet of paper (or a reminder file in your smartphone), list your key brand descriptors. Refer to this list daily to keep you "on brand."

Ecosystem

Step 4: Ecosystem

Ecosystem: Leverage Influencers to Establish Brand

Gloria, the procurement director from chapter 3, was worried after her company was acquired. Her counterpart from the acquiring company began taking over functions that previously had been her group's responsibility. If he succeeded in his power grab, she could lose her job.

Her immediate boss understood Gloria's value, but other influential executives did not know her well. She needed to be more visible to these executives and make her value known. She volunteered to lead the development of the strategic plan. She wanted to demonstrate her strategic leadership, and set up interviews with each of her executive stakeholders for a discussion of the key issues. At the end of each interview, she explained that ambiguity about roles and responsibilities at her level were causing internal confusion. She made her case for retaining her pre-integration role.

By Gloria's educating the influencers, her boss heard not just from Gloria but also from other executives that her leadership role in procurement should remain unchallenged. Gloria succeeded in developing a more strategic and higher-profile brand image with executives, thereby safeguarding her job. She leveraged her internal brand ecosystem to achieve her goal.

Taking It to the People

You are now at Branding Step 4, and are well on your way in your self-branding journey. You should now have an understanding of:

- Who you are (your assessment of yourself and other's perceptions)

- What unique value you provide (positioning statement)

- The desired brand to achieve your goals (brand strategy platform)

- How to represent and message your rational value, or cake, and emotional value, or icing (messages and key brand descriptors)

Next, you have to decide who should receive your brand messages. Branding is not just about what you say, it's what others say about you. That's where the ecosystem comes into play.

You have limited time and resources. You cannot talk to everyone, nor should you. You need to prioritize. Developing an ecosystem model will help you to focus on the people and organizations that will have the greatest impact on your success.

What Is the Brand Ecosystem?

Think of the brand ecosystem as spheres of influence that create perceptions about your brand (Figure 5.1).

> We can message and promote our brands, but, in the end, it's what others say about us that determines how we are perceived.

The old adage that "perception is reality" has never been truer than in branding.

When Hillary Freeman ran for City Council, she needed to educate key influencers about who she was and what she stood for. She created positive word of mouth among influencers in the neighborhood groups, business community and special interest groups as a desirable council candidate. She had an ecosystem model and she worked it successfully. We will look at Hillary's ecosystem model shortly, but first we need to define the brand ecosystem.

Figure 5.1
Brand Ecosystem Model

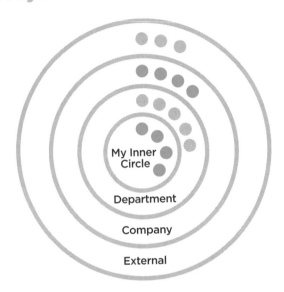

The brand ecosystem consists of spheres of influence that create perceptions about your brand. Figure 5.1 shows a simple ecosystem model where you are at the center, your group or department is the next sphere, then the company at large, ending with the external world. The ecosystem model can also be represented as a pie wedge cut from these concentric circles, so that it looks like an inverted pyramid (see Figure 5.2).

The brand ecosystem is a model for brand references and for communication. This important branding step provides a systematic way to:

- Develop your brand ecosystem model

- Understand the path of reference-checking and communication

- Identify your key influencers or potential partners

- Determine win-win goals, challenges and actions to manage influencer relationships

When you are a candidate for a job or a leadership opportunity, your ecosystem references are key to your credibility. When you are looking for funding, venture capitalists engage in "due diligence" interviews with your ecosystem to ensure that you are what you say are.

Anytime there is perceived risk in a decision to hire, partner or fund, the ecosystem will play an important role in providing third-party feedback.

Imagine that you needed back surgery. It's unlikely you would choose your surgeon randomly—the stakes are too high. You would probably ask for recommendations from other doctors, friends and family, and you'd likely do online research on the backgrounds and consumer ratings of surgeon candidates. Only then would you feel reassured that you were choosing the right surgeon. Likewise, when you apply for a job or try to get funded, others will seek ecosystem reassurance. They don't want to risk their reputations or business outcomes on someone whose background or ideas cannot be verified.

The 90/10 Rule

The best way to establish and enhance your brand is by leveraging the power of the influencers in your brand ecosystem. Who are the influencers? Generally, 90 percent of the market is influenced by a few—the 10 percent who we call the influencers. They are the people we trust to help us determine which doctor to choose, which person to hire and whether we should invest in a company or not. In the case of the Internet with its broad reach, the influencers could represent less than 1 percent of the market.

The reason why so many companies want celebrities to promote their products is because celebrities have sway over the opinions of their many fans. Oprah Winfrey, the television celebrity and former talk-show host, has tremendous power to create demand for anything she endorses. Her recommendations have turned books into instant bestsellers. Her followers think, "If Oprah says it's good, it must be." On the Internet, there are bloggers and trendsetters who are highly influential with their followers. Have you ever been swayed to try a product based on an Internet recommendation by a friend or a blogger you trust? I will readily try out new smartphone apps based on the opinion of a few social media friends. You are probably an influencer within a certain ecosystem sphere, even if it is only with friends and family. In certain companies, the opinions of a handful of employees can make or break reputations. Think about who the influencers are in your company or market.

A key to personal branding is leveraging the right ecosystem model to reach your goal

The Brand Ecosystem Model

Your goal determines what your ecosystem model looks like. Let's say your goal is to switch careers from engineering to marketing. Your engineering ecosystem will have a different set of influencers than your marketing ecosystem. If you are a retail executive and your goal is to become an outside board member in another industry, you will need to develop an external ecosystem that identifies business influencers in this new industry.

Those who need to partner or find new opportunities within their companies should focus on an internal ecosystem model, which models the influencers inside their company. Conversely, job hunters, entrepreneurs and independent consultants need to develop an external ecosystem model.

Look at the ecosystem model in Figure 5.2.

Figure 5.2

Ecosystem Wedge Model

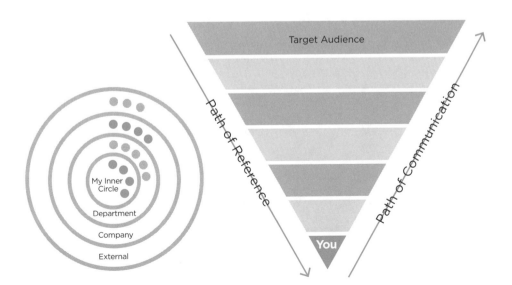

The Ecosystem Wedge Model is a "pie slice" view of the concentric circles that make up the ecosystem. How you communicate—your **path of communication**—should move out from those influencers closest to you to the wider public. People close to you need to know first! In between you and your target audience are influencers from various groups. How people check your references—**path of reference**—is generally by moving through the ecosystem from your target audience (the outermost sphere) to you. However, your target audience may choose different reference points at random. Reference checking does not necessarily follow a serial path through the ecosystem.

To make the ecosystem model easier to fill out, we have taken a wedge out of our concentric spheres of influence. You need to be in the apex of the pie slice, or wedge, and your target audience for branding is in the outermost sphere. For each sphere, identify a group of influencers. For a consultant's external ecosystem model, the next spheres could be partners, key clients, complementary service firms, professional organizations and media, ending with potential clients in the outermost sphere (see Figure 5.3). Next, identify individual influencers in those groups. Your influencers may be people who are quoted or featured in the media, are retweeted frequently, speak before groups, lead professional organizations, shape opinions through word-of-mouth references or have other influence over your career. You'll brainstorm your list and prioritize later. Voilà! You have your ecosystem model.

Figure 5.3

Ecosystem Wedge Model for Consultant

If you decided to get married, for instance, you would probably tell your family and friends first because if your mom learned about your engagement from strangers, you might lose your biggest supporter. The same is true of your personal brand. If you are launching a new personal brand, you need to get feedback, buy-in and endorsements from those closest to you in your ecosystem before going out to a wider audience. Those seeking references on you will check with key individuals or groups in your ecosystem. If those closest to you cannot corroborate your value messages or ideas, your credibility will suffer. If the ecosystem backs you up, then establishing your brand accelerates.

Let us examine the external ecosystem model of City Council candidate Hillary Freeman. In chapter 4, we learned how Hillary branded from the inside out— from her core values to the brand promise that she delivered to voters. The ecosystem is also about branding from the inside out. In the ecosystem model, we start with insiders and work outward to our potential audience or customer.

Figure 5.4

Hillary Freeman Ecosystem Model

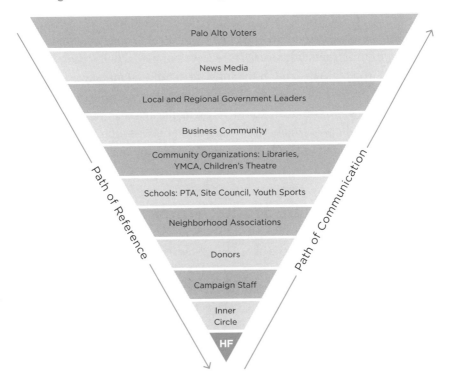

Hillary's goal was to win a seat on the City Council. Her target audience was Palo Alto voters. If Hillary were a company, the target audience would be potential customers. If Hillary wanted to get a job, her target audience would be recruiters and hiring managers. The target audience should be in the outermost sphere of the ecosystem model. The person who is branding is shown in the apex of the wedge.

Hillary's inner circle was her "kitchen cabinet"—a small group of her closest advisors. Before any public announcements or outreach, Hillary and her advisors ensured that her campaign staff understood her brand positioning. Empowered with the key messages and brand strategy, the campaign was able to represent her with consistent branding and communications. Hillary also gathered endorsements from key donors and supporters before taking her message out. She had a ready reference structure before going to the neighborhood groups, the school community, community organizations, the business community, government leaders and the news media. Hillary worked the ecosystem in a systematic way to win over the constituencies who would advocate for her and influence the electorate to vote for her. As we revealed in chapter 2, Hillary won with the highest margin of votes of any candidate and won her place on the City Council. She couldn't have done this without the support of the ecosystem.

In chapter 3, we discussed how you need to have value messages that resonate with different audiences. The ecosystem model helps you to understand which groups and individuals need tailored messages. For instance, Hillary communicated to library supporters her role in advocating for a bond measure to renovate the city's aging libraries. To the schools community, she emphasized better cooperation between the city and the school district on land use and adding sports fields for youth.

External Ecosystem Model: Professional Services

We will go back to our example of reference checking to select a back surgeon. In the surgeon's ecosystem model (Figure 5.5), you are the "potential patient" and you may look to any of the references between you and the back surgeon to determine if she is the right surgeon for you. You want to choose a surgeon whose reputation is upheld by multiple trusted sources. Let's say the surgeon you are considering has gone to excellent medical schools and is board certified, but has some negative reviews for "bedside manner" on consumer rating sites. However, your trusted family physician and your next-door neighbor say this surgeon is the best. You rate the trustworthiness of your family doctor and neighbor over consumers whom you have never met, and you choose the recommended surgeon.

Figure 5.5

Ecosystem Model for Surgeon

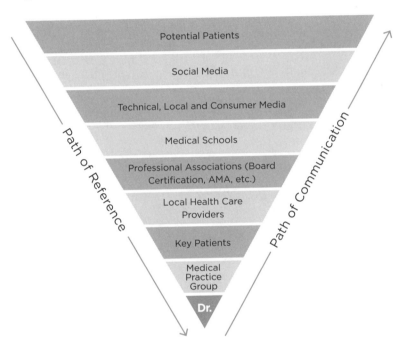

We've seen how a patient can use the ecosystem to find a surgeon. But how might our back surgeon use her ecosystem model to launch a new service? She has developed a new, minimally invasive technique for back surgery that lowers surgery risks and patient recovery time. We'll call it the Pil Technique, named after her. She wants to let consumers know about it. Should her first move be to advertise it? The answer is no.

Why not? Remember, back surgery is perceived as a high-risk procedure. Awareness alone will not move patients to try something risky without ecosystem assurance. Bypassing the influencers by advertising directly to consumers will not succeed. Once the Pil Technique is advertised, the reference checking begins. If the key influencers don't know about the technique or raise doubts about the procedure, the brand of the Pil Technique and its creator will suffer.

The best course of action is to follow the ecosystem path of communication. You brief those closest to you first, and expand your market education out from this base of support. Only after lining up credible references from key ecosystem groups should Dr. Pil advertise her technique. With the ecosystem creating buzz and advocating for her, it is likely that Dr. Pil will not have to advertise at all.

Imagine having influencers advocate for you. When a trusted person recommends that a company hire you, you will have a distinct advantage over someone who lacks a similar endorsement. Entrepreneurial companies that are introduced to venture capitalists by VC influencers, such as another successful entrepreneur, get immediate consideration versus entrepreneurs who lack an introduction.

You are not alone in branding yourself.

> **Your ecosystem acts as a marketing and sales team that can catapult your brand from unknown to desired.**

See the Hillary Freeman success example if you doubt the power of the ecosystem.

Internal Ecosystem Model

Paul is a principal engineer at a global manufacturing company. He was tasked with driving key initiatives that integrate engineering systems and quality systems.

Paul decided he needed to brand his key initiatives team and partner with key groups to be successful. He developed an internal ecosystem model (Figure 5.6) and placed Executive Leadership, his ultimate audience for branding, in the outermost sphere.

Figure 5.6

Paul's Ecosystem Model for Initiatives

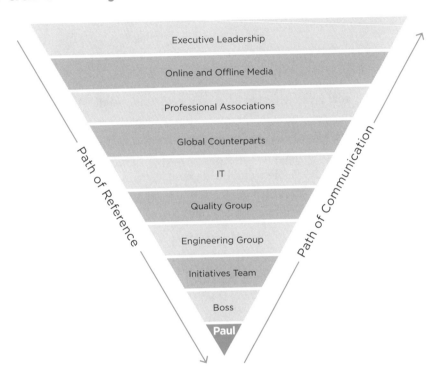

His inner circle included his boss and the early members of the key initiatives team, which he planned to augment with teams for each of the initiatives. Being part of U.S. operations, he included three U.S. groups next: engineering, quality and IT. Next he added the global counterparts to the U.S. groups. Finally, he added some external groups to his ecosystem model—professional associations and online and offline media, since both can influence brands internally.

He held an offsite meeting with his executive sponsors and with key stakeholders. The purpose was to kick off the engineering and quality initiatives and to educate the group on the objectives. His value messages for each audience resonated. He built strong leadership teams for each initiative. The initiatives were successful and he educated internally (U.S. and global operations) and externally (professional associations and technical media) on these best practices. His boss and top executives recognized him for his leadership success and for enhancing the company brand.

In Paul's case, the ecosystem model was a way to get things done (recruit and build the initiative teams) and a way to educate on the team brand and his individual brand.

Job Search Ecosystem

As always, your goal will determine what your ecosystem model should look like. This generic model is a good start for any job search, but the actual organizations and individuals you identify in the different spheres will vary depending on what kind of job you seek, in what industries and in what geographies. Leverage social media presence to help recruiters and hiring managers find you. However, one of the best ways to get a job is through friends who tell you of an opening in their company and recommend you for the position.

Figure 5.7

Ecosystem System Model for Job Search

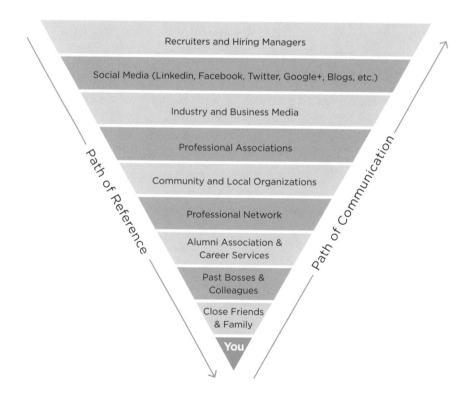

Take Time for Relationship Building

Ellen was a typical Type A manager who was results-driven. She was so concerned about meeting deadlines that she didn't take the time to develop relationships—not with her team, her colleagues or senior leadership. In fact, she admitted that her team rejoiced when she left the office because her brusque and efficient manner put them on edge. She was concerned about why others were being promoted over her, even though her accomplishments were more significant. Doing a good job is not enough, I told her, adding that shared social experiences go a long way toward building a bond of trust and likability. When we explored the role of the ecosystem and the importance of ecosystem relationships to branding, it was as if a light bulb went off in her head. "Wow, I get it," she said. She realized that office social events and visits were not a waste of time, but were an important opportunity to develop relationships with colleagues in a more relaxed environment. She decided that the only way to make relationships happen was to schedule them into her calendar, which she did. Ellen raised her visibility and likability quotient with her influencers, and has since been promoted.

Four Keys to Strong Ecosystem Relationships

There are four keys to making and keeping strong ecosystem relationships:

1. Common bond and likability
2. Two-way value
3. Ongoing communications
4. Relationship management

Let us take a more detailed look at each of these four areas.

Common Bond and Likability

You will not always be liked by or have a common bond with all of your influencers. But connecting on some level is important. I remember being seated on a plane with an entrepreneur I didn't know. Small talk led to a discussion of his acting hobby and my admission that I had once dabbled in theater. We had a laugh about onstage goof-ups, and then circled around to our professional backgrounds. He will now remember me not only as a branding expert but someone with whom he shared theater stories. Strong cake and icing can be a powerful mnemonic.

I've worked with a number of executives on personal branding who seem to think that social banter is a time waster. They are very goal-oriented and just want to "cut to the chase" and do business. However, they need to understand that the warm-up chat before discussing weightier topics is extremely important. Think of this social interchange as the on-ramp to the freeway of business discussions. It's dangerous to jump into 70-mile-an-hour traffic starting from zero without accelerating to traffic speed. During "on-ramp" small talk, people size each other up and decide if they like and trust their conversation partners. In France, it is considered somewhat rude to talk about business during a meal. Only after one enjoys the meal and the mealtime conversation should business enter into the equation. In other countries, the social sharing of tea or coffee might be the precursor to a business discussion. You can jeopardize your ultimate business goal by skipping the "on-ramp." Learn the art of conversation and how to be engaging socially to get the most out of your ecosystem relationships.

Two-Way Value

The ecosystem is about give and take. It is not a one-way street where you do all the talking and the taking.

I remember a former colleague who asked me for a meeting to see if she should become an independent consultant. I bought her lunch, gave her some valuable tips and connected her with some others I thought could help. She went on to become a successful consultant, but I never heard back from her—no thanks and no updates. It is doubtful that I will ever recommend her again. When the value flows in only one direction, influencers are less likely to want to help you.

If you are looking for a job (Figure 5.7) or new business, it is fine to call on others with the hope of an introduction, a lead or helpful information. However, the relationship will be more powerful if there is a two-way exchange of value. Ask yourself, "What value do I have to offer?" It may be a follow-up email with an article of interest, a connection or the sharing of your expertise. Don't forget to close the loop to let those who have helped you know if you got the job or made the recommended connection. At the very least, make sure you thank your connections for their help.

Ongoing Communications

If influencers are important to your brand, you need to keep them briefed on your value and progress. You also need to check in to see how they are doing. If people hear from you only every couple of years, it's unlikely that they will know your current brand and be able to help you. Do not wait until you need something to reach out to people. Have a relationship that is based on mutual interest, not just need.

Relationship Management

We will be talking about relationship management later in this chapter. For now, the important point is to be proactive in guiding perceptions about your brand. Successful management encompasses understanding your key influencers, developing a win/win relationship and growing the relationship over time.

Identifying Influencers

Once you have modeled your ecosystem, you need to name the individual influencers in each group. Narrow down your influencers to only a few individuals for each group to keep it workable.

If you are feeling overwhelmed, use the Top Influencers Scorecard and just identify five top influencers (Figure 5.8).

Figure 5.8

Top Influencers Scorecard

Rank	Influencers	Rating	Challenge	Goal
1				
2				
3				
4				
5				

Rate how well influencers support you and your ideas on a scale of 1 to 5, with 1 being "work against you" and 5 being "enthusiastically support." I call this the "friends or foes" rating.

If your goal is to change careers or move into a new position, your influencers may not be that familiar with you. This scorecard will make it clear what relationships you need to work on.

Remember the 90/10 rule. Only a small number of individuals will influence the many about your brand. The goal is to move these influencers to become your advocates, or at least to neutralize them if they are detractors.

What are influencer relationship challenges? Common challenges include lack of awareness, misperceptions, dislike or negative associations.

What are appropriate influencer relationship goals? Your relationship goals can be: Move the dial from a "2" to a "3," get an endorsement or testimonial, partner on a project, approve a proposal, get promoted, or change a negative opinion.

Managing Your Ecosystem Relationships (Optional Tool)

Awareness of your brand ecosystem will help you to be more effective and use your time more wisely as you build your personal brand. For some, completing their ecosystem model is enough. For others, using more detailed and systematic management tools is preferred. If you work better with greater granularity, you can put your ecosystem influencers into a spreadsheet or a customer relationship management (CRM) tool, or use the templates that are shared in this section.

If an influencer relationship is important to you, it deserves to be nurtured and managed over time. Ecosystem relationship management helps to establish priorities, goals, actions and measurement for important relationships. This optional management tool (Figure 5.9) is especially helpful when mapping out how to launch a new initiative or idea.

Figure 5.9

Ecosystem Relationship Management

Ecosystem Sphere	Company or Group Name	Individual Name	Tier Rating*	Friend or Foe Rating**	Goals	Next Steps	Due

* Tier ratings are for understanding how important each influencer is. For instance, Tier Ones might always get your important news from you in person or with a personal call, and Tier Twos might get a personalized email.

** Friend or Foe Ratings should be on a scale of 1 to 5, with 1 being hostile to you and with 5 being an enthusiastic advocate. The goal will be to improve these ratings over time.

Figure 5.10

Sample

Ecosystem Relationship Management

Ecosystem Sphere	Company or Group Name	Individual Name	Tier Rating*	Friend or Foe Rating**	Goals	Next Steps	Due
Customers	Past Client	Ellen James	1	5	Get testimonial quote	Phone call or meeting	Feb-10
Financial Services	Money Manager	Joe Smith	1	3	Partner on marketing event. Move to a 4 rating.	Meeting to propose event participation	Feb-10
Media	Metro Business	Lou Tran	1	3	Feature article. Move to a 4 rating.	Email pitch, then meeting	Mar-15

A Word About Networking

The brand ecosystem is about building and managing an ecosystem of two-way value that helps you reach your brand goals. Why don't I just call it networking? Because networking can have negative connotations if it is done without a strategy and without authenticity.

Many people think that the greater number of contacts through networking, the better. By some measures this is true, since you can lower the degrees of separation from your targets the more people you know. That is a driving force behind LinkedIn, the professional network. However, I would rather have a smaller number of people who know me well and who care about me than a host of people for whom I am a mere business card with no emotional connection.

Think of all those business people who play golf for hours together. They are not just getting exercise, they are sharing interests, friendship and business destinies. The proverbial Old Boys' Network, where men help their buddies in business, is very much a social club. Men seem to understand this. Women, less so. Ellen, who had the "Ah ha!" that she needed to develop more meaningful work relationships, finally got it and no longer viewed socializing as a waste of time.

The purpose of too many networking events seems to be to exchange as many business cards as possible.

> It makes sense to know a broad network of people, but the key is to develop a relationship.

If you are busy doing "speed dating" at an event, it's unlikely that you'll develop any meaningful relationships. I encourage professionals to give of themselves without demanding or expecting anything in return. A golden phrase that everybody loves to hear is: "How can I help you?" If you are genuine and follow through, others will likely reciprocate.

The key to networking is to be liked and to be remembered. The first is important, for as I said in chapter 1, no one will advocate for you who doesn't like you. The reason why I like people may have more to do with their personalities and their presence (icing) than with their profession (cake). Do you recall my memorable experience with the entrepreneur who liked acting? My second point on being remembered is critical. If no one can associate you with something of value or interest, your business card will be tossed.

Many people who are shy and lack confidence in crowds dread networking events. You'll usually find them in a corner with their drink, watching others have conversations. My advice is to put your focus on helping others to connect, which will help you forget about your own insecurities. Make it a point to introduce yourself to people who are off by themselves, and later connect them to someone else who might share their interests. You'll be a hero to them. By acting more like a host, you'll feel more confident and empowered.

In sum, the brand ecosystem model and relationship management provide a strategic framework for focused relationship building and communications. It is much more powerful than mere networking.

Chapter 5 Summary

- You need to leverage your brand ecosystem to establish credibility for your brand.

- The brand ecosystem consists of spheres of influence that create perceptions about your brand. It identifies the path of reference-checking and the path of communications.

- 90/10 Rule: A small number influence the many.

- Four keys to making and keeping strong ecosystem relationships are 1) common bond and likability, 2) two-way value, 3) ongoing communications and 4) relationship management.

- You need to leverage the right ecosystem to reach your goal.

- In the end, it's not what you say but what others say about you that determines your reputation.

- Your ecosystem acts as a marketing and sales team that can catapult your brand from unknown to desired

Chapter 5 Action List

o   Based on your goal, create a model of your ecosystem using the Ecosystem Wedge Model in Fig. 5.2.

o   Name the key influencers for each sphere (e.g., influencers in your department, the company at large, professional organizations, media, etc.).

o   Narrow the list down to a manageable list for each sphere.

o   Fill out the Top Influencers Scorecard in Fig. 5.8.

o   OPTIONAL: For more advanced work, fill out the Ecosystem Relationship Management chart in Fig 5.9. You can use the fields in Fig. 5.9 in a spreadsheet for easier manipulation.

Action Plan

Step 5: Action Plan

Build Your Brand Action Plan

A couple of years ago, Alison, a corporate lawyer in a large company, got a new boss. A self-described good presenter, Alison, unfortunately, was not at her best during her first presentation in front of him. He made a snap judgment that this was a weakness of hers. In addition, he seemed to think that she was just a generalist when it came to corporate law.

Alison realized she had a branding problem. If she wanted to get the recognition and the opportunities that she desired, she had to reinvent her brand in the eyes of her boss and those around him. She applied the BrandingPays System and worked to change perceptions of her brand.

First, she determined her positioning differentiation. She realized she could combine her legal specialty, business background and experience in the firm's technology to set her apart. Alison positioned herself as an intellectual property (IP) specialist who could strategically manage the technology patent portfolio from both a legal and business standpoint. In short, her positioning goal became the Strategic IP Lawyer.

When she compared her current brand to her desired brand in the Brand Strategy Platform, she recognized that she needed to work on collaboration skills and upgrade to a more professional look that commanded greater authority.

Alison's priority action was to change the negative opinion her boss held about her presentation skills and her differentiated value. She volunteered to do multiple presentations on strategic IP management to both technology and business groups in the company as well as professional organizations. She made sure that her boss saw her in action. She developed compelling presentations tailored to her audiences that demonstrated her strategic business and IP expertise. By sharing her knowledge with different groups, she underscored her collaborative attitude. She got people to take another look at her both because of a sleeker professional wardrobe and because she backed it up with content and a strong delivery.

Within three months of implementing her new brand, Alison's boss praised her in his staff meeting for her great presentations, her collaboration within the company and her strategic contributions in managing the company's patent portfolio. Within a year, Alison got her promotion. Branding does pay!

A 360-Degree Brand

Alison achieved her goal by implementing her positioning and brand strategy through a Brand Action Plan, the fifth step in the BrandingPays System. The brand action plan will help you to deliver a 360-degree brand—a clear and consistent delivery of your brand through all communications, gestures and actions.

By following the BrandingPays System, you have completed your 1) positioning, 2) messaging, 3) brand strategy and 4) ecosystem. You now have all the ingredients for your cake and icing. Now you will finalize the recipe.

We have divided the Brand Action Plan into two courses of action: brand improvement and brand communication. Brand improvement will help you to improve on those areas necessary for delivering on your brand promise. In other words, if you want to be a spice cake and lack spice, you can take action to remedy this deficiency in brand improvement. Brand communication ensures that you build awareness and recognition for your brand by communicating your cake and icing.

Let's take a more detailed look at what goes into brand improvement, and how we define actions for brand communication.

Brand Improvement

Brand improvement focuses on filling the gaps between your current brand strategy platform and your desired brand strategy platform that you completed in chapter 4. Let's revisit sections of our Brand Strategy Platform to see a sampling of brand improvements for some of our individual branding examples.

Figure 6.1

Strengths
(Cake)

Hard Skills

Soft Skills

Expertise

←Hard Skills. Bob, the unemployed computer programmer, needed to develop more skills in the area of web software development. He can take courses, read technical books and do pro bono programming to gain these skills.

←Soft Skills. Eileen, who wanted to become vice president of marketing, needed to work on her collaboration and leadership skills. She can work with an executive coach, take courses, read business books and look for opportunities to learn from others.

←Expertise. Marnie, who wanted to be an elder care sales specialist, had to volunteer, network and do Internet research to gain the expertise and experience she needed to change careers from retail sales.

Figure 6.2

Personality
(Icing)

Personality Attributes

Type of leader, worker, friend

Brand Metaphor

←Personality. Eileen needed to create a more empathetic personality to be more effective in a collaborative corporate culture. She can work with her executive coach or mentor on this change.

Figure 6.3

Brand Image
(Cake & Icing)

Brand
Associations

External Image

Relationship
Image

←**External Image.** Alison, the corporate lawyer, upgraded her wardrobe, got a sleeker and more professional hairstyle and projected more confidence to enhance being seen as the strategic IP lawyer that she was.

Figure 6.4

Brand Promise
(Cake & Icing)

Rational Value

Emotional Value

Brand Experience

←**Brand Experience.** Candidate Hillary's brand promise included "solving problems with citizen engagement," so she needed to increase her opportunities to LISTEN and learn from residents.

Figure 6.5 is a sample brand improvement template. As you look at the gaps between your current brand and desired brand in the Brand Strategy Platform, you will recognize areas where you need to improve. I have populated this brand improvement template with some areas that are key to strong brands. However, you can customize the Key Areas to Improve column to the specific areas in which you need work.

Figure 6.5

Brand Improvement Template

Key Areas to Improve	Rating (How am I perceived)	Challenge	Priority Actions	Allies or Tools
Visibility and Understanding of My Brand/Value				
Strategic Leadership				
Presentations				
Social Interactions				
Personal Style/ Image				

To give you an idea of what a high-level brand improvement plan might look like, see Fig. 6.6. The Rating column should be filled with a number, with 1 indicating very low achievement and 5, very high achievement. This number should reflect how you are currently perceived based on your own assessment and feedback from others. Over time, your goal should be to raise all of your scores to a 4 or 5.

Put what may be holding you back in the Challenge column. In Priority Actions, list a few key actions you can take to change your behavior and people's perceptions of you. In Allies and Tools, identify the BrandingPays tool and other people and resources who could help you to make the improvements you seek.

Figure 6.6

Sample Brand Improvement Plan

Key Areas to Improve	Rating (How am I Perceived?)	Challenge	Priority Actions	Allies or Tools
Visibility and understanding of my brand/value	1	Low awareness among key influencers	--Develop key influencers --Share expertise in presentations --Social media program	--Ecosystem Model --Top Influencer Scorecard --Messages
Strategic Leadership	3	Lack strategic leadership image	--Volunteer for strategy initiatives --Training	--Work with mentor or executive coach
Presentations	3	Lack presence	--Training --Present often to build skills	--Presentation skills coach
Social Interactions	2	Have some social anxiety	--Practice reaching out to others --Smile	--Social anxiety therapy --Work with mentor or coach
Personal Style/Image	2	Casual style hinders global exec image	--Global culture training --Upgrade professional appearance	--Personal Brand Strategy Platform --Image consultant

Brand Communication

Once you have a credible foundation for delivering on your brand, you can embark on your brand communication plan. Does this mean that you need to address all areas of brand improvement before communicating your new brand? No, but you do need a minimal set of evidence to be credible. If your desired brand is to be a collaborative leader and you are acting like a lone cowboy, you need to work on your collaboration skills and opportunities.

The elements of your brand communication program will be different from another person's because you have a unique set of circumstances driving your actions. These include your goal, target audience, positioning, desired brand, strengths, current perceptions, ecosystem and environment. Don't think of communications as a checklist of standard items. Let your strategy drive your tactics. If you have a short-term goal influenced by only a handful of people in your company, you should focus on direct communication with these influencers rather than doing a broad communications program. However, if your goal is to boost your visibility in the industry to increase your career opportunities, you will need to broaden your reach.

Four Phases of Brand Communication Using the Ecosystem Model (Advanced)

The Four Phases of Brand Communication model (Figure 6.7) will help you to develop a brand communication plan that engages different parts of the ecosystem depending on the phase. This brand communication model has been proven successful with both product and company launches throughout my career in Silicon Valley. It works equally well when you are reinventing (or launching) your personal brand.

The Regis McKenna Inc. team that handled Apple product launches introduced me to a version of the Four Phases model. If you wonder how companies successfully get key influencers to say good things about their products when they launch, pay attention to this model. Think of yourself as a product to be launched. You need to 1) validate your "product" concept, 2) build a reference or partner structure, 3) have influencers give their endorsements publicly when you launch and 4) communicate evidence of your momentum and success.

> **A phased model for communicating your personal brand is very helpful in understanding whom to talk to, when, what to say, and how to establish and maintain your brand leadership.**

The first two phases are done in private to ensure that your value messages are compelling to your target audience, and to build the reference structure that you'll need to be credible with your brand communications.

The second two phases are the public phases, and apply to when your brand is made public, when references publicly support you and when you continue to build your leadership position with additional announcements and evidence.

Different parts of the ecosystem are more important at different phases of communication. Note that early on, you need to concentrate on those influencers who are closer to you in terms of their stakeholder relationship. In Phase 4, others may try to copy your leadership claims, so you will need to continue to raise the bar of leadership through new ideas, thought leadership, achievements and other evidence that show your momentum. If you are repositioning, introducing a new initiative or launching something new, you will need to repeat these four phases.

Figure 6.7

Four Phases of Brand Communication Using the Ecosystem Model

Let's examine what goes into the Four Phases. The colored layers conceptually indicate the ecosystem focus of each phase. As we mentioned, the model is divided in half, with Private Activities on the left and Public Activities on the right.

Four Phases of Brand Communication

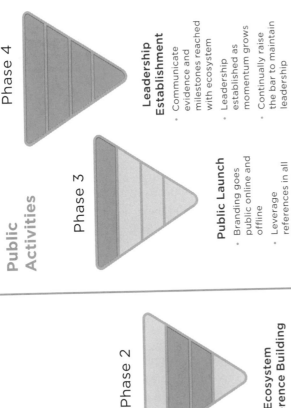

Private Activities

Public Activities

Phase 1

Validation

- Solicit feedback on your positioning and key messages
- Refine positioning and messages based on feedback
- Process develops buy-in from advisors who feel ownership in your success

Phase 2

Ecosystem Reference Building

- Communicate positioning with ecosystem influencers
- Final revisions to messages based on input
- Get approval to use them as references

Phase 3

Public Launch

- Branding goes public online and offline
- Leverage references in all communications
- Monitor launch response and course correct as necessary

Phase 4

Leadership Establishment

- Communicate evidence and milestones reached with ecosystem
- Leadership established as momentum grows
- Continually raise the bar to maintain leadership
- Repeat Four Phases when repositioning or launching something new

Figure 6.8

Private Activities

Phase 1: Validation

Ecosystem Focus	Purpose	Channel	Materials or Other
Your inner circle and friendly influencers	Private feedback of your positioning and messages (or symbols and images or Ecosystem Model)	In person is preferred, but video chat or conferencing works especially well with digital media influencers	Might include a short presentation, a video, a website layout, a logo design, a draft of a profile or a vision

The validation phase provides an excellent opportunity to see if your category and value proposition resonates with people, and if your messaging is compelling. With Hillary Freeman, the City Council candidate, we used early meetings to refine her messages and build support for her candidacy. Sometimes during this process, your early influencers will not agree with your ideas and messages. Although you will ultimately make the call on what you communicate, be sure to be open to change—especially if the feedback is consistently negative.

The validation meetings should be done one-on-one for optimized two-way idea exchange. You'll recognize the type of response instantly if people are nodding their heads and agreeing, or if they frown and looked confused. You need to probe to understand their concerns and ask their advice. By helping you, they are investing in you and your ideas. If you incorporate their suggestions (provided that they have sound advice), and update them, they will want to root for your success.

Figure 6.9

Phase 2: Ecosystem Reference Building

Ecosystem Focus	Purpose	Channel	Materials or Other
Same as Phase I, but adding more influencers	Educate influencers and get approval to use as references	As appropriate (in-person meetings recommended for key influencers who have not met with you in Phase I, but email or social media may work for your inner circle or friendly influencers)	Near-final materials (based on revisions from Phase I input)

During Phase 2, you'll go back to your friendly influencers to update them on your latest strategy, messages and images. You will also expand your briefings to other influencers and solicit them as references or for testimonials.

It is flattering to know that you have helped people create a better "product" because of your input. Your first instinct is generally to redouble efforts to help them be successful, because you've invested some of yourself in the endeavor—even if it is only by offering some friendly advice.

When I was in advertising and market consulting, we used to joke that engineering just wanted to throw their products over the wall and advertise them without any understanding of customer need or any market conditioning. Phases 1 and 2 (the private phases) are about doing the groundwork to align with customer needs. Conditioning the market by seeding references is key to credibility.

Let's say that you want to reinvent your personal brand from being a banking executive to a consultant helping social entrepreneurs. If your messaging is that business and banking experience can help social enterprises, then you would want 1) references from banking that validated your expertise and ability to help social entrepreneurs and 2) social entrepreneurs who say how financial understanding and connections are what they need.

Phase 2 is about seeding the "market" to ensure acceptance of your new brand or ideas. You are building a reference structure so when your brand goes public, a key set of influencers will endorse your new brand.

Figure 6.9

Phase 3: Public Launch

Ecosystem Focus	Purpose	Channel	Materials or Other
Your target audience (or potential customers)	Educate on your new brand or ideas	Indirect, Social Media (possibly other media if you are launching a new product or service)	Final materials/digital media

With your new personal brand, you might be launching a website, a blog or a thought leadership program, putting up a new LinkedIn profile or applying for a new job. The "launch" will not be a one-day event, but rather a shortened time frame when you get a critical mass of attention. It might involve a coordinated social media program with guest blogs, podcasts, an introductory video, a campaign to build Twitter followers and Facebook friends, and proliferation of your content and good ideas. If you aren't adept at social media, at least email all your contacts with links and a short blurb that paraphrases your new profile copy for, say, LinkedIn. Let people know how they can engage with you and, if appropriate, help you.

You can help get your endorsers to be your references by adding their quotes—for instance, statements agreeing with your vision—to your blog posts or guest blogs. If you are going to be interviewed on a podcast or other media, you can supply the interviewer with a few of your pre-briefed contacts. I always have quotes from clients on my website, in addition to my recommendations on LinkedIn. In this way, I can facilitate the ecosystem reference-checking and build credibility faster for my brand.

The key to a successful launch is to condition the market to accept your new brand by lining up key influencers as references *before* the public launch. Remember, promoting new products or your personal brand only causes the market to seek assurance from the ecosystem. Lining up key endorsements in advance will speed establishment of your desired brand.

Figure 6.10

Phase 4: Leadership Establishment

Ecosystem Focus	Purpose	Channel	Materials or Other
Entire ecosystem	Build and reinforce leadership position	All channels	New and existing content

If you have been successful in your public launch, then a broader audience is aware of your brand and has been influenced to think about it in a positive light. Your influencers have been vocal and supportive. People have begun talking about you offline and online, accurately reflecting your brand positioning. You have been contacted about new opportunities for jobs, partnerships, business, funding, publicity or speaking.

Now what? Resist the urge to rest on your laurels. Positioning is a dynamic process. Although you may be seen as a leader of your chosen category today, tomorrow a competitor may knock you off your perch or the market may shift and no longer need your unique talents. You need to innovate continually and raise the standard for providing value.

When I relaunched my brand as BrandingPays (formerly Karen Kang Consulting) in January 2010, I followed my own methodology by testing messages and lining up references in advance. My newsletter announced the change of name and brand identity, but assured everyone that the quality and methodology remained unchanged. My website was completely redesigned to be more personable and interactive. My blog started focusing more on personal branding. I gave a series of public and private presentations with the new brand identity, and people in my seminars started referring me to other groups. Within 18 months of launching, I had more than 20 invitations to speak on personal branding, from the London Business School to Genentech, from Vistage International to national conventions. The buzz began with my brand launch, but I had to deliver on my brand promise to keep the word-of-mouth momentum going. The truth is that once you lay claim to a leadership position, you need to deliver the evidence. That's why Phase 4 is about continuing the momentum, evidence delivery and innovation.

Brand Action Example

Think back to Mike, our open software leader for the graphical web. He had been positioned as a leader in desktop graphics, but technology and market shifts changed everything. He had to reposition himself for leadership in a new category with a new ecosystem.

Mike's Goal: Reposition brand from leadership in desktop graphical software to leadership in open software for the graphical web

Mike's Brand Action Plan

Brand Improvement

- Understand graphical web trends and both business and technical issues.

- Learn new open source technologies and programming languages

- Temper authoritarian style and grow collaborative leadership skills (especially important for leading open source organizations with many members who have different agendas)

Ecosystem Management

- Volunteer for leadership positions with open source technology initiatives

- Build relationships with influencers in open source and graphical web ecosystems

- Attend (or host) social gatherings of like-minded technologists where Mike's engaging sense of humor and storytelling ability will help to create better bonds

Brand Communication

- Update profile with new brand positioning for LinkedIn and other social media

- Align résumé with new brand positioning

- Speak at open source and graphical web conferences on market needs and how open source technology can address these needs

- Speak inside company to various technology and product groups on how to leverage open source initiatives

- Write blog and white papers for open source organizations

- Build following on social media with interesting posts and information on open source and graphical web software

Mike is now positioned as a visionary leader in open software for the graphical web both inside his company and in the industry. He deliberately chose to reinvent his brand. Mike's cake relies heavily on his technical understanding and vision, and his icing is anchored by an engaging personality. A self-admitted nerd, he is well groomed but doesn't spend a lot of time thinking about his wardrobe. As a matter of fact, if he were too fashionable, the other technologists might look at him askance.

The BrandingPays System has its roots in the product and company positioning work that I have done for the past two decades. Company examples, such as Biosys below, are useful illustrations of differentiation and messaging strategies that individuals can undertake to reinvent their own brands.

Lessons from Rebranding an Entrepreneurial Company

Biosys, a small company in the agricultural biotech industry, was on the verge of bankruptcy due to poor positioning on multiple fronts—market positioning, company positioning and technology positioning. Customers did not understand the market that Biosys served or the company's technological value, and neither did potential investors. How could tiny Biosys compete against the giant agrichemical companies that were developing their own biological pesticide lines? The giants were competing in the crowded market for pesticides that targeted leaf-eating insects. Biosys, on the other hand, had a biological product that killed pests in the soil. Regis McKenna, my then boss, and I divided the market into an above-ground segment and a below-ground segment. Biosys could credibly compete in the subterranean market segment that had few competitors. The estimated $4 billion segment for underground biological pesticides was large enough for this start-up's initial market.

Unfortunately, Biosys was not well positioned as a technology company—a real negative for Silicon Valley investors. The company had a reputation as "dirt worm farmers" due to confusing positioning and messaging. We helped Biosys to reposition itself as an agricultural biotech company using proprietary genetic technology. The new message: Biosys develops beneficial nematodes (microscopic organisms) with customized genetics to "seek and destroy" underground pests.

The company lacked the "hot company" image that start-ups needed to get funded. We got the buzz going for Biosys by holding an invitation-only event at the company's offices. The main purpose was to reintroduce Biosys to the investment community and other influencers as a technology company with great prospects. Museum-like poster displays told the story of the market need, segmentation and technology. Scientists in white lab coats explained the custom genetics used and demonstrated the proprietary production techniques. At the white-tent catered affair, luminaries and current partners extolled Biosys's virtues, then the well-coached president presented the company story and opportunity to an enthusiastic crowd.

The upshot? Within a week of the event, Biosys had two investment bankers vying to take the company public. Six months later, Biosys raised $30 million in its initial public offering. Not bad for a bunch of "dirt worm farmers."

A Word of Advice for Entrepreneurs

Your personal brand as a founder is highly dependent on the brand positioning for your company and vice versa. If your company has a poor image, it will reflect badly on you. Your company positioning and messaging must be clear. Likewise, if your personal brand as a leader lacks the vision, passion and drive to be successful, few will want to follow.

If you are seeking funding, tell your company story in a compelling way and engage investors in your vision. Let both your company brand and personal brand shine. At the reintroduction event, Biosys was true to its brand strategy, from the messaging and the visual branding to the caliber of event guests and ambiance. The clear strategy empowered every employee and partner to represent Biosys well. You have the same opportunity to shape your company's brand and to be seen as the chief evangelist and visionary. Don't hide behind other executives.

Investors want the founder to sell them on the vision. Remember, if you want to come across as a strong entrepreneur, bring your company story alive with a clear strategy and compelling marketing opportunity. Entrepreneurs with a good idea but who lack passion and drive will find it hard to get funded. You need both cake and icing.

Chapter 6 Summary

- Your brand action plan should include both brand improvement (areas you should improve to deliver on your brand promise) and brand communication (activities to build awareness and recognition of your brand).

- The Four Phases of Brand Communication Model provides a guide to the goals and ecosystem emphasis during the private and public stages of your brand launch and communication.

- If you are an entrepreneur, your company's brand positioning and messaging must be clear. Likewise, if your personal brand as a leader lacks the vision, passion and drive to make it happen, few will want to follow.

Chapter 6 Action List

o   High-Level Planning. Take a look at your key brand descriptors (chapter 4) and develop a short list of high-level actions that will enable you to deliver on this brand. If you don't have time for a detailed plan, this is a quick way to help you get going.

o   Detailed Brand Action Plan. Build out activities for your brand improvement and brand communication.

  -   Brand Improvement. Note the gaps between your filled-out Brand Strategy Platform for your current brand and your desired brand. Fill out the Brand Strategy Improvement Template to keep track of how you will improve and your progress.

  -   Brand Communication. As appropriate, use the Four Phases of Brand Communication to help you map out the ecosystem focus and activities to establish a leadership position and a credible brand.

o   Keep focused. Write down your three top priority actions for the next 30 days.

360-Degree Branding:
Vision, Symbols, Words and Deeds

360-Degree Branding: Vision, Symbols, Words and Deeds

The Care2 Story: Rebranding from the Inside Out

When Randy Paynter was 11 years old, he traveled with his ornithologist dad up the Amazon River. The richness and diversity of wildlife, vegetation and people of the deep jungle made a lasting impression. He was concerned about the destruction of the Amazonian rain forests and wanted to do something to help. With the advent of the Internet, he found a way. He started a website called Care2 that would bring social activists together to make a difference in the world.

Over time, the website became the number-one petition site in the world. However, it added so many community features, e-cards, healthy and green living content and news feeds that it eventually became cluttered and hard to navigate. The company had lost its way in how to define and express its brand. This caused market confusion and hampered Care2's efforts to grow its membership and its revenue base.

When I was brought in to help the company, it had something no other competitor could boast: *Care2 was the world's largest and most trusted social action network*. Care2 needed to claim and establish this leadership position.

Its brand promise was enabling members to

- Feel good about taking social action in a friendly community.

- Make informed choices affecting your health, sustainability and the world.

The original Care2 logo was designed in four colors and incorporated an endangered Amazon tree frog with bulging orange eyes. The green frog overemphasized Care2's environmental roots and no longer reflected its broader umbrella of causes. The gangly amphibian appealed more to men than to the women, who made up the larger share of the membership.

Figure 7.1
Care2 Original Logo

Energy Energy Design, a visual branding firm headed by Creative Director Leslie Guidice, partnered with me on the Care2 project. Energy Energy
redesigned the company logo and the website to underscore the new brand
message. In the new four-color design, butterflies rise out of the logotype to
symbolize how individual actions can lead to profound change. According
to Care2, the "butterfly effect" in physics references "the flap of a butterfly's wings in the Brazilian rain forest, that moves the air, that redirects the
breeze, that alters the wind, and eventually leads to a hurricane moving up
the east coast of America." For years, Care2 had given butterfly symbols to
members each time they took social actions. Therefore butterflies, which are
women-friendly and evoke community better than a lone frog, became the
new symbol for Care2.

Figure 7.2
Care2 Redesigned Logo

Care2's brand finally made sense, and CEO Randy Paynter felt empowered by the alignment with the company's history and its current vision. The CEO followed the company's brand ecosystem model (chapter 5) and went to the Care2 employees before telling the rest of the world about the rebranding. He wanted employees to know that branding, which goes far beyond the visual design, starts with the company's soul and is demonstrated through its actions. He said to his staff during the internal launch:

> Let's all ask ourselves, "What am I doing to deliver our brand promise to our members? What am I doing to deliver on our value proposition to nonprofit partners and corporate sponsors? Are my actions consistent with what our brand is all about?"

Employees embraced the new branding and changed the website to reflect the new priorities and messaging. The brand was rolled out to influencers, then to the rest of the world.

By all measures, the rebranding was a success.

Before launching the brand change, Care2 had 8 million members. Less than a year later, its membership grew by 50 percent to 12 million. Today, three years later, Care2 has 20 million members and counting. It is a brand that delivers on its brand promise and continues to build interest and loyalty. Here are personal branding lessons that individuals can draw from the Care2 example:

- **Align your brand with your core values.** CEO Randy Paynter could passionately represent his company because the company mission was aligned with his own values. If what you do does not match your core values, you won't be or be seen as authentic.

- **Understand your target audience and meet their needs.** Care2 recognized that women interested in adopting a healthy lifestyle, and in taking small actions to help the world, were a large part of its membership. The company took steps to make the website, content and community friendlier to this demographic. In marketing, we talk about understanding and having empathy for the customer. Try to see the world from your target audience's eyes to understand what you need to do to meet their needs.

- **Make implementation priorities and direction clear with strong positioning and brand strategy.** Care2 was able to leverage their brand strategy and message document with employees, marketing and design consultants and other service providers to ensure smoother execution. Unlike a company, you may not be using outside help to implement your brand. But once you have your strategy set, you'll better understand what tactics will get you to your goal. Without a strategy, it's like shooting without a target.

- **Message and represent your brand consistently.** In Care2's case, the images and easy website navigation were as important as the words. The company didn't just say the site was simple and friendly; Care2 demonstrated it in the user experience. The words you use, the way you dress and the manner in which you engage others are part of the brand experience that you impart. Ask: "Am I on brand?"

- **Understand and leverage the ecosystem.** Care2 reached out to employees, nonprofit partners, corporate advertisers and key community members in advance to ensure that the right buzz and endorsements built credibility and interest before the brand relaunch. You can also do ecosystem education to raise your credibility and create a word-of-mouth environment that will accelerate acceptance of your new brand.

- Continue to innovate to maintain leadership positioning. Care2 has added Daily Deals for socially responsible products and butterfly credits that can be earned for your favorite cause. The company maintains its leadership because it finds new ways to add value and to differentiate its brand. What new ideas or initiatives can you be known for that will continue to underscore your leadership?

Care2 is a great example of 360-degree branding from the inside out. What follows are specific areas that you can master as you live, represent and communicate your brand.

Vision or Thought Leadership Branding

As Randy Paynter and the Care2 story show, a strong vision can be the driving force behind your brand and brand actions. Often the vision provides the value, emotional connection and best association for your brand.

For entrepreneurs, your vision for the industry and your company is worth as much to investors as the actual product idea and current implementation.

For company managers, your vision for culture, leadership and the industry may largely determine how high you rise in the organization.

For recent MBAs, your fresh vision and ideas may be the new blood that companies seek when they look to hire.

Let's see how Libby, a recent MBA graduate, has reinvented her brand and crafted a new vision to help differentiate her value. Libby didn't wait until graduation to rebrand herself as an entrepreneur. As a matter of fact, she has reinvented her brand a few times in her young career. She has repositioned her brand from being known as a print editor to a digital editor to a social media consultant to a digital community entrepreneur. She made it happen by learning new areas, volunteering, blogging on her expertise and engaging with influencers in new ecosystems. She has been active on key social media platforms like Twitter and Facebook, and has blended her online persona with in-person engagement at digital, innovation and entrepreneurial conferences.

When it came time to attract investor funding for her company, she was so intent on explaining the technology and product features (cake) that she lost sight of the emotional connection to investors (icing). Libby is not unlike so many entrepreneurs who are enthralled with their product or technology but lose sight of the emotional side of their brand. Where is the passion for making a difference in the world? What is the big idea?

We worked together to emphasize a vision that would resonate on both an intellectual and an emotional level with customers and investors. Her company was not just offering up a digital community with curated events and jobs, but was enabling a new trend toward blending the worlds of work and life for creative digital and technology people. Her goal: Mesh cool local events and people from different disciplines to inspire new ideas, companies and partnerships. She has embarked on a program to evangelize her vision of creative collaboration through work-life blending with blogging, speaking at conferences and engaging the influencers. Libby is the face of this vision and her company enables it—city by city. She has aligned her personal brand with her company brand. In the process, she has created an emotional, aspirational connection, as all entrepreneurs should for strong branding.

Realtors in the residential real estate market face difficulty differentiating in an area that has become oversaturated with sales agents all claiming similar experience. Thought leadership expressed in a methodology that you own can set you apart. Michael, the owner of a boutique realty company in an affluent area of California, has developed a unique methodology for the premium pricing of residential real estate. Developing a methodology, productizing it and branding it can go a long way toward making an intangible (service) into something tangible (product). We've helped numerous professional services companies, executives and consultants to develop and brand processes to help differentiate themselves from competitors.

Michael's branded methodology coupled with his expertise and experience in the sales of luxury homes on the private market has made him unique in the industry. He blogs on related topics, and has been quoted as an expert in leading business publications and local media. His thought leadership brand reflects well on his company, attracting the best realtors and well-qualified clients. In turn, his company's continued growth and success helps provide positive evidence for his personal brand.

Your Look, Your Image: The Basics

Those who already have the fundamentals of how to present themselves through their external image may skip this section. However, even if you think you have your act together in terms of your external style, it makes sense to peruse this section and consider carefully whether everything you are doing today best represents your brand.

Remember that strong branding is a marriage of cake (rational value) and icing (emotional value). Business generally places the highest value on cake. But, as economist D. S. Hamermesh documents in his book *Beauty Pays: Why Attractive People Are More Successful*[4], attractive people get paid more and get more opportunities.

There is more evidence that presenting an attractive image in the context of your business environment is important. In *Impressive First Impressions,* authors Vu H. Pham and Lisa Miyake cite studies where participants took only milliseconds to form impressions of faces (39 milliseconds)[5] or websites (90 milliseconds)[6]. People often make snap judgments based on initial images or impressions.

We cannot all be tall, thin and beautiful. However, we can present an attractive image no matter what our size, shape or physical attributes. Think of your body and your face as a canvas. What are the colors, textures and symbols that can represent your values and personality? How can you present an attractive image?

Posture and carriage. Let's start with your posture and how you carry yourself. If you stand tall, you will come across as more confident. A slumping posture, besides potentially leading to health problems, gives the appearance of indifference, lack of confidence or even depression. People who sit erect at a conference table or who lean forward slightly look awake and engaged. Walk tall and carry yourself with pride if you want respect from others.

4. Hamermesh, D. S., *Beauty Pays: Why Attractive People Are More Successful* (Princeton, NJ: Princeton University Press, 2011).
5. Pham, Vu H., and Miyake, Lisa, Impressive First Impressions (Santa Barbara, CA: Praeger, ABC-CLIO, LLC) xiv.
6. *Ibid.*, xviii.

Attitude and well-being. A positive attitude is attractive. A negative one is not. There may be legitimate times to let people know if you are feeling down, but, for the most part, keep your feelings about being tired or being put upon at work or home to yourself. Your boss, clients or colleagues want to hear about solutions, not problems.

Try to live a healthy life by eating right, exercising and managing stress (yoga, meditation and being in nature can help). No one will want to give you a challenging job or to fund your company if you seem to be sinking mentally, physically or emotionally. If you look in the mirror and see bright eyes in a smiling face, you are radiating well-being.

Be kind and respect others. Treating others how you would like to be treated is common courtesy. Listen to what others have to say, show empathy and help them out if you can. Small acts of kindness done with authenticity can bond people to you for life, creating brand loyalty.

Respect for others includes respecting their time. Be punctual. Be concise in your communications, including emails and phone messages. Organize your thoughts in advance. Use bullets in emails and call attention to deadlines or action items. Your recipients will appreciate your getting to the point, whether it is in written or spoken communications.

Hair. A well-done hairstyle can enhance your image. (See chapter 8 for more on hair for profile photos.) A neat, contemporary cut will underscore your professionalism and modern sensibilities. Most hair salons will give you a free consultation, so take advantage of this offer to get a professional opinion on the optimal cut for your hair.

Face. For women, well-applied facial makeup can help to create a more pleasing image. (See makeup tips for photos in chapter 8.) If you have features and skin tone that make you seem washed out, you may blend into your work environment. You need to be visible to make your brand known. Judicious application of some foundation, blush, mascara and lipstick can help you to stand out in a positive way. Avoid an overly made-up look, as it will look unnatural. Ask a makeup professional to help if you are unsure of what to do.

Grooming, scents and perfume. Good grooming is essential for making a positive impression. Even if you are a software genius, maintaining good grooming habits will enhance your opportunities.

- Many people have allergic reactions to perfumes and colognes, so if you do use a scent, make sure it is lightly applied.

- Showering daily and wearing deodorant should keep away any negative scents (!).

- Brush and floss your teeth, and use mouthwash to ensure that your smile and your breath are pleasing. It's hard to appear businesslike with spinach between your teeth, so floss after meals, if necessary. After eating spicy meals, it may be wise to brush your teeth and to use breath mints. When I was in Korea, where a pungent pickle called *kimchi* is eaten regularly, I noticed that nearly every woman in the office building brushed her teeth after lunch.

Wardrobe. American humorist and writer Mark Twain was making a joke when he said, "The clothes make the man," but, there is truth to this. When a man or woman walks confidently into a room in a fine, well-tailored suit with shoes and accessories to match, the natural reaction is: "Wow!" Yet some company cultures are decidedly casual and such dress would be out of place. It's important to understand the context and culture of where you are doing business to decide what is appropriate dress and what is not.

Another popular saying, "When in Rome, do as the Romans do," comes to mind when I think about what people wear. A mid-level U.S. executive who traveled to Switzerland on business shocked her European colleagues by wearing jeans to her last day of meetings there. Her rationale was that she had to leave for the airport immediately after the meetings ended and wanted to be comfortable on the plane ride home. You can be sure that how she dressed distracted from the points she wanted to make, and probably contributed to her reputation as a rude American not well suited for a global executive role. Showing sensitivity and adaptability to different cultures is important in any company—especially a global one.

If your company is into casual dress (such as jeans and T-shirts) and you want to fit in but still maintain a more professional look, consider wearing dark blue jeans and cropped jackets. Going casual does not have to mean unkempt T-shirts, dirty gym shoes and frayed jeans. I like the term "geek chic," meaning a casual style with a fashion edge.

I truly believe that beauty starts inside of you and radiates out. If you are at peace with your values and have a passion for life and your ideas, people will be attracted to you. You will radiate a positive vibe and confidence. What you wear can enhance your attractiveness, but it's what's in your soul that is most important.

Branding in Multimedia

Posting podcasts, videos and presentations online is a popular way to get your brand recognized by a wide audience. However, make sure that these formats enhance your image. Today, many people are putting up do-it-yourself content on the web. Using a smartphone or a laptop with a video cam, people can instantly add video to their social media posts. Although viewers are forgiving when it comes to on-the-go photos or video postings, a video résumé or video brochure should have better production value. Unfortunately, I have seen some video résumés that hurt rather than helped the chances of the job candidates.

Bad lighting that casts you in shadows can make you look more like a criminal than a professional manager. A rambling elevator pitch punctuated by too many ums and ahs, fidgeting hands and nervous blinking can cast doubt on your presence and communications capability. You don't have to memorize a speech, but do write down and remember your key talking points (See chapter 3).

If you have a naturally high-pitched voice, try lowering it. If you speak in a monotone, try modulating your voice to sound more interesting. Smile while you talk and your voice will naturally sound more lively.

To come across confidently, you need to look directly at the lens of the video camera. You can color in a black circle, tape it to your wall and practice looking at it while you go through your key talking points. Then, start practicing in front of a video camera. Do 20 takes of your elevator pitch until you get it to sound natural.

The most important thing in video is connecting with your audience. Imagine talking to real people, friends who are interested in what you say. As a song made popular by Louis Armstrong goes: "When you're smiling . . . the whole world smiles with you." It couldn't be more true!

Presentations

When you present—whether in your company or at an outside event—your brand is on center stage, so make the most of it.

All of the earlier suggestions about how to look, smile and use your voice to effect in photos, videos and audio apply to presentations. Think of 360-degree branding.

I have coached a number of the mid-level executives who wanted to be seen as more strategic. Presentations are an excellent way to demonstrate strategic thinking. Say that you have to do a progress report to executives on an initiative you are leading. Doing a one-slide intro that graphically depicts the corporate objective that your initiative helps to achieve, or a slide that shows the driving trends, will show that you see the big picture. Instead of diving into the details of implementation, lay out the initiative graphically with a colorful chart showing key milestones.

Your presentation should follow the "inverted pyramid" approach of general or high-level ideas followed by key points and evidence details. Thoughtful organization will make your presentation easier to understand and show that you have a strategic and analytical mind.

If you need tips on how to put together and execute a great presentation, there are a number of good books to consult. Check out the Further Reading section at the end of this book.

Business Cards and Documents

What does your business card say about you? If your company has issued you a business card, you don't have much say in how you come across except for your title and contact information. But, if you are an entrepreneur or consultant, your business card should be designed to communicate your brand.

Company name: Is your company name memorable, easy to say and spell, and does it enhance your brand awareness and brand promise? Not all company names will satisfy all criteria for a good name, but if you have an opportunity to choose a company name, try to select one that will help your brand.

Logo: Is your logo creative and attractive? Is it aligned with your brand?

Font: Is the font easy to read in all formats—print, web, black-and-white and color? Does it have a more contemporary look, like those found in sans serif typefaces such as Helvetica, or is it a serif font such as Times Roman? Many designers can create a custom logotype, which is a unique font, for your logo. For those in marketing or creative areas, custom logotypes reinforce your expertise and creative values.

Colors: What does your color palette say about you? Soft pastels are associated with feminine qualities. Red and black seem more masculine. Grays and dark blues look more corporate. There is no steadfast rule when it comes to colors, but it would make sense to choose a different palette from your competitors so that you stand out. A good designer can show you a number of color palettes—main colors with accent colors.

Paper stock: When you hand out your business card, people will feel the weight of the stock. If your card is made of flimsy paper, it will give the appearance of a business that can't afford better card stock or that doesn't care about quality. Your designer or printer can guide you on the best choice of paper for your business card or other printed pieces.

Printing: You do not have to pay for an expensive offset printing process to have a quality business card. Professional printing services offer digital printers that achieve excellent printing results at a reasonable cost. Your business card is important in setting a first impression and could be referenced afterward. Make sure that the printing quality represents your brand.

Documents: Whether your documents live in digital form or are printed, ensure that they reflect well on your brand. Check for attractiveness and consistency of design and fonts, and correct spelling and grammar. Edit your documents so that the writing is concise and that the flow is logical. A document with good content will be enhanced by strong design and editing.

Chapter 7 Summary

- A vision or thought leadership can provide the value, emotional connection and best association for your brand.

- Presenting an attractive image in the context of your business environment is important.

- Areas that help to set your image and brand include:

  - Posture and carriage, handshake, attitude and well-being, kindness and respect, hair, face and makeup, grooming and scents, wardrobe, accessories
  - Multimedia, including presentations
  - Business cards and documents

Chapter 7 Action List

Do an inventory of the items listed in the Summary under "Areas that help to set your image and brand." Note areas that are not in alignment with your desired brand and add these to your plan for brand improvement (chapter 6).

Portable Branding and Social Media:
Getting Started

Portable Branding and Social Media: Getting Started

The social media tips in this section are for beginners, since I have encountered so many professionals and entrepreneurs who need the basics. If you are already proficient in social media, this chapter can be a reminder to align your online persona and activities with your brand strategy, or you can skip this chapter entirely.

The BrandingPays System focuses on developing your strategies and messages for a compelling brand. Social media is a tactic, but many people think personal branding and social media are nearly synonymous.

"I tweet, therefore, I brand."

True to an extent, but the real question is: Will you be known for the right things? So many people in social media are sending out mixed signals that make their brands unclear. People that I follow on Twitter tweet on specific topics. Through the consistency of their messages, they have built credibility as experts. However, there are many more who tweet on any subject under the sun. Yes, they have ubiquitous tweets, but there is little value for their followers, unless you like random posts.

> **Social networking through digital means is here to stay.**

Even if you are late to the game, now is as good a time as ever to jump in. Every day things are changing in social media—there are new platforms, new ways that people are connecting and sharing. The rules are being rewritten while we speak.

If you aren't convinced that you need a social brand—that is, a brand in social media—please read on.

Why You Need to Be in Social Media

If you are looking for a job or other opportunities, it is critical that you be found. So many of my clients have been hired after recruiters found them on LinkedIn. A publisher found me on LinkedIn, checked out my blog and asked me to write a book on branding. I didn't choose this publisher for my book, but it does illustrate that having a presence in social networking opens you to a world of opportunities. People looking for your experience or talents can find you.

According to Jobvite's online survey[7] of more than 800 human resources and recruitment professionals in the United States:

- 89 percent use or planned to use social networking for recruiting

- LinkedIn is the most dominant platform for social recruiting (87 percent usage), followed by Facebook (55 percent usage) and Twitter (46 percent usage)

- 64 percent use or planned to use two or more social networks for recruiting and 40 percent use or planned to use three or more social networks for recruiting

Even if you are not looking for a job, you can be sure that your clients, colleagues, investors or others are looking at your LinkedIn page or doing a Google search on you. If you can't be found or show up poorly, you may lose an important opportunity.

Choose Your Social Networks

Be selective about how you choose your social networks and how you brand on them. There are many social networks, but if you have limited time and resources, I would stick to the Big Three (with the caveat to grab your online real estate on Google+):

---

7. Jobvite 2011 Social Recruiting Survey Results <http://web.jobvite.com/rs/jobvite/images/Jobvite-SRP-2011.pdf>.

- LinkedIn

- Facebook

- Twitter

My advice is to start with LinkedIn, and you can build from there.

LinkedIn

LinkedIn is the social network for professionals. You need to have a complete profile on LinkedIn if you are serious about your career. I will touch on a few key areas that are important to establishing your differentiated brand on this network.

Your LinkedIn Title

If you are looking for a job or new opportunities, use a title that provides more compelling information than just your current job title and company. See the old versus new example below:

Old	Vice President of Corporate Marketing Widget3, Inc.

The title doesn't indicate any differentiation and the company, if not widely known, does little to enhance the personal brand.

New	Corporate Marketing Executive—Enterprise and Consumer Software Strategic Corporate Branding, Integrated Marketing Programs, and Change Management Leadership

This marketing executive is differentiated by his software expertise and leadership in change management, a skill that companies undergoing culture change because of a merger, acquisition or new management will value. The strategic corporate branding and integrated marketing are included as necessary skills for a VP of corporate marketing but not necessarily differentiating. His profile will include evidence and metrics that back up his brand positioning claims.

Your Profile and Chronological Experience

Your profile is one of the best ways to guide your brand and position your unique value with prospective employers, partners, clients or others. See chapter 3 for an example of Celia's messaging in her LinkedIn profile.

Don't forget to add keywords that recruiters will search, and achievement highlights that will provide credibility for your positioning claims. Recruiters and others will search using keywords for certain experience and expertise. For technical people, it could be software languages. For managers, it could be global, language or key management skills.

A civil engineering manager went from zero LinkedIn inquiries to several each month after he revised his profile. He positioned himself as a:

Consulting Engineering Manager for Civil and Environmental Infrastructure—for municipal clients and private companies

His title cued recruiters that he is an engineering manager who has experience valuable to an engineering consulting firm that specializes in civil and environmental infrastructure projects. He included such keywords in his profile as "planning, design and construction administration" as well as such terms as "business development, project management, client management, risk management and quality assurance." This engineer came up multiple times for different search criteria.

Recommendations

Your brand is based on what others say about you, so the Recommendations section in LinkedIn is important to your credibility. LinkedIn makes it very easy to send requests for recommendations. I usually ask for a LinkedIn recommendation at the end of a consulting assignment when clients say I've done great work. "Would you mind putting that in a LinkedIn reference?" I'll ask. Invariably they say yes, and then I send them a LinkedIn request with a few ideas on what their recommendation might include. If they are busy, I'll ask if I can paraphrase what they just told me verbally and send it to them as a draft.

It makes sense to meet clients in person or to call them before sending a reference request. Connecting personally will give you an opportunity to refresh their memories (if necessary) on what you worked on together and the results. Your meeting will also afford you an opportunity to update them on your current positioning. Do show interest in their updates and ask how you can help them in their pursuits. Perhaps you can recommend them on LinkedIn.

Groups

You probably already have networks within LinkedIn. By virtue of your membership or association with these groups, you will have more credibility in these networks. You should add your viewpoints to existing discussions or start your own. Follow the discussions for a while before jumping in so that you understand the etiquette of posting in each group. Examples of LinkedIn groups you can join include:

- Colleges and universities where you are an alumnus or alumna

- Professional organizations (e.g., Interactive & Digital Media Group and American Marketing Association)

- Special interest groups (e.g., Nonfiction Authors Network and BlogHer)

If there isn't a group with your interest or expertise, consider starting your own LinkedIn group. It is an instant way to position yourself as an expert and as someone who is giving back by organizing a group that will benefit those who share your interests.

Links

Be sure to include personal branding URLs here, such as Twitter, Facebook, your blog, your website, your YouTube channel or other sites. One of my clients had several links with different names that served to confuse her brand. We cleaned up her links and included only those that reinforced her brand name.

The more complete you can make your LinkedIn profile, the better for being found in searches and providing a rounded view of your personal brand.

Facebook

Facebook is a network that blends your social life and, if you allow it, your work life on one platform.

Whereas LinkedIn is a more buttoned-down view of you (mainly your cake), Facebook allows a more rounded picture (more icing).

You can control who sees your posts, friends, photos and profile, but do know that recruiters and hiring companies can find creative ways to get access to your full Facebook persona.

According to a Reppler survey of 300 hiring professionals, 91 percent said they use social networking sites to screen job candidates. Therefore, even if you think Facebook is for only friends and family, prospective employers will check to see how you show up in social media. Your Facebook page provides clues to your character, values and judgment.

A more shocking statistic from the Reppler survey is that 69 percent of respondents said that they rejected candidates based on content found on the candidate's social networking profile. Being tagged in a bachelor party photo drinking alcohol with scantily clad women may not be the image that you want a prospective employer or client to see. Likewise, a prospective employer or investor may be offended by your political rant on social media. "But, I want to be my authentic self," you say. There are plenty of opportunities to show your authentic self and personality that won't put off potential employers. Make a conscious choice each time you post. If you wonder whether this could come back to haunt you, it is probably a good idea to share this thought or photo in person rather than through social media.

If you want to open up your Facebook network beyond friends and family to your business acquaintances and others, you will want to use the Facebook privacy controls, which are not very user-friendly. TIP (based on Facebook's user interface at time of researching this book): Click on the Facebook logo to get to the home page, and select "Friends," then click on "MORE." On the Friends page, you can click on the "Create Lists" button to segment your Facebook audiences. Then, before you post on Facebook, you can use the Friends drop-down menu to choose the lists to which you want to post.

In addition to your personal page, you can have a Facebook page for your business. People are interested in interacting with people, not faceless companies, so the more you can do to put a human face on your business page, the better. Showing real people in videos and photos, and commenting in personable language on posts, will humanize your company and underscore your values. Be careful about using your Facebook business page solely for promoting your products—no one wants to feel sold to constantly. It is fine to run promotions via Facebook, but you also need to provide informational and entertainment value. Give people a reason to "like" your page and to want to return. Keep the content fresh, engaging and valuable.

Twitter

Twitter is a micro-blogging network that allows you to post "tweets" of 140 characters. You can follow people whose posts you like and others can follow you. Many are attracted to the real-time nature of Twitter streams, which allow you to follow hot trending subjects and discover fresh information on topics that interest you. I use Twitter to bolster my "branding guru" image. Therefore, I tweet almost exclusively about branding topics—both corporate branding and personal branding.

Do you have to use Twitter to have an online personal brand? No, but it is a lot easier to gain followers on Twitter than it is with your personal blog, which could take some time to build a following.

> Focusing 90 percent of your tweets on business or your area of expertise, and 10 percent on personal tweets, is probably a good rule of thumb.

If you currently have a Twitter account and have not used it effectively for personal branding, consider repositioning yourself on Twitter by changing your profile to emphasize your focus (mainly cake, with some icing). Then, tweet accordingly. Follow some Twitter influencers in your chosen space, retweet their posts and engage them in conversation as appropriate. Their followers and other people who share your interests will find you, and you will grow your following. Don't forget to follow people back and comment on or retweet their tweets. When people retweet your Twitter postings, it is common courtesy to thank them publicly, thereby giving them more Twitter exposure.

You can use hashtags to help folks follow the conversation around a certain topic, such as #brandingpays, or an event. Often organizers of my speaking events will notify attendees of the hashtag for the event so participants can tweet their thoughts or quotes during my talk. If you want to check out existing hashtags, go to www.hashtag.org.

There are many tools that can help you to manage your Twitter account. I like using HootSuite, a tool that lets me see all of the topics and people I am following in a visual dashboard. HootSuite allows me to send my posts to Twitter, Facebook, LinkedIn, Google+ and other social networks separately or simultaneously. This tool will allow you to schedule your posts so that they will automatically be sent throughout the day or even weeks ahead (especially useful if you have evergreen content that can be spread out over time). If you post frequently and consistently about your topic of choice, you will become known in that space. You will gain a reputation and enhance your brand.

Google+

Google+ is a newer social networking platform that many social media influencers, such as best-selling author Guy Kawasaki, are advocating. It's like a cross between Facebook and Twitter, and enables easy segmenting of your posts to different "circles."

Guy Kawasaki said on a talk show that Facebook is about talking to the people you went to high school with and Google+ is about talking to the people you wished you went to high school with.[8] That may be a simplistic and not totally accurate view, but it does differentiate Facebook's origins of being school-friend-centric.

However, a BrandingPays pulse survey[9] of 384 professionals (mainly in Silicon Valley) found that Facebook and LinkedIn were by far the most prevalent networks used for personal branding. Of our respondents, 51 percent said they use Facebook all the time or often, and some 41 percent said the same of LinkedIn. Likewise, 12 percent said they never used LinkedIn and 16 percent said they never used Facebook. However, 61 percent of respondents said they never used Google+ for personal branding. We'll see how this changes over time.

Even if your mainstream audience is not on Google+, they will be eventually. Why? Because Google is the big gorilla of search. If you want to be found, you should have some presence on Google+. At the very least, grab your personal Google URL, which is a great segue to my next section.

---

8. *Gavin Newsom Show,* Current TV, May 25, 2012.
9. BrandingPays Pulse Survey, January 2012. <http://brandingpays.com/brandingpays-pulse-survey-january-2012/>

Own Your Online Real Estate

Your name is a huge part of your brand. If people don't remember your name, you aren't doing a good job of branding.

You need to own your online real estate—that is, your name online or your vanity URL. If you haven't already done so, sign up on LinkedIn, Facebook and Twitter, using your full name (or some combination if your name is already in use) in your URL. Here is how my brand name shows up in key URLs:

LinkedIn URL

LinkedIn.com/in/karenkang

If you don't have a personal website or blog, you can reference your LinkedIn URL. Make sure the URL contains your name (or some variation on it if it is already taken).

Facebook URL

Faceboook.com/karenkang.brand
Facebook.com/BrandingPays

I originally opened my Facebook account as Karen Kang Consulting, which was before I rebranded as BrandingPays. When I decided to be Karen Kang on Facebook, that URL was taken, so I opted for karenkang.brand. That way, people will find my name with the "brand" designation that will clue them that this Karen Kang is actually me. For my company and book activities, I use my Facebook page account: facebook.com/BrandingPays.

Note: Facebook will let you change your URL once in your lifetime, so think twice before you make the change. If you are in doubt, test the potential URL change with friends or someone you trust before changing it.

Twitter handle

@karenkang

I like to have a human face on my Twitter account. I tweet out branding information and engage with my followers. I have toyed with the idea of using a BrandingPays Twitter account, but have opted to discuss my book and speaking events under my @karenkang account. The main reasons are for streamlining administration and avoiding duplication.

Google+ URL

gplus.to/karenkang

I am sure that Google will eventually allow Google+ users to have vanity URLs, but currently your Google+ ID is a long string of numbers—not very user friendly for business cards or email signatures. To get a shortened vanity URL using your name, you can go to a third-party service like http://gplus.to/ and sign up for your "Nickname," as they call it.

Website URL

Brandingpays.com (previously, kang.com)

If you have a company, get a URL that includes your company name followed by .com, or .org if you are a nonprofit organization. Emails should be from YourName@YourCompany.com. I got the kang.com domain (out of a million people with the Kang surname!) in 1994, and with it, the perfect email address: karen@kang.com. Now that I have my brandingpays.com URL, I go by karenkang@brandingpays.com. I choose to use my full name because that is an important part of my personal brand.

For personal branding, try to register your full name as your domain, as in FirstNameLastName.com. If it is not available, you can try variations like your first initial and last name, or FirstNameMiddleNameLastName.com. This will help you to rank higher in search results for your name.

Here is how I use some of my BrandingPays URLs:

BrandingPays.com My main company site for consulting, training and coaching.

BrandingPays.com/blog My BrandingPays blog.

BrandingPays.com/book The site for my BrandingPays book, events and shopping cart.

As you can see, I am reinforcing the BrandingPays brand in each of these URLs for different offerings of content and activities.

Your Google Search Results

Right now, do a Google search on your name. What do you find?

Hopefully, you show up several times in the first page of the search results. A search may show up images (such as profile photos of you), websites (such as your LinkedIn profile, blog and personal website), video (such as your YouTube posts), articles, news releases, reviews, and on and on. People who have search page results look like they matter to the world. People who don't appear in search results seem like nonentities. Nearly every employer expects management candidates to have social media understanding, since this is the way the world communicates and influences today.

> You need to guide your own social image as it reflects on your professionalism and your competence in navigating modern realities.

Your Avatar

In social media, your avatar (a photo or illustration that is your personal visual identity) is synonymous with your brand. I encourage people to use the same avatar on all their social media platforms. If you use several different avatars, you are diluting the branding effect. For professionals (unless you are an artist), a photo is preferable to an illustration. Pick one photo that represents you well and use it consistently.

Your brand is highly portable in social media. To ensure your avatar shows up when you comment on blogs, you can register it at a third-party service, such as Gravatar (stands for globally recognized avatar) at https://en.gravatar.com.

When I browse my Twitter streams, I look for familiar faces. I have friends who are constantly changing their Twitter photos. It makes me work doubly hard to find them, since searching a name is much slower than visual recognition.

People will have a hard time remembering your brand if you are changing it frequently. Imagine that your favorite consumer brands changed their logo, colors and design every month—how would your recognize them in the store? As in consumer branding, personal brands become recognized faster with consistency and frequency. Therefore, choose one good profile photo for use on all your social networks.

Here is a checklist to evaluate your choice of avatar photo:

Clarity. Is the photo clear and in focus? A grainy photo from your last vacation will not present you in a professional light. Consider paying a professional to take your photo.

Lighting. Does the lighting enhance your look? Bad lighting that highlights dark circles under the eyes, that washes out your complexion or that makes you look sinister will detract from the positive aspects of your brand. A professional will light interior shots to avoid shadows, or choose the most flattering time of day for an outdoor shot.

Smile. Do you have a genuine smile? A closed-mouth smile is not as inviting as a broad smile. In a wonderful book called, *Enchantment,* author Guy Kawasaki promotes the eye-crinkling Duchenne smile[10] that will aid your likability. A smile will connect you in a positive way with viewers. It's the fastest way to put icing on your brand.

Hair. Is your hair neat and professional? Pay for a well-recommended hair salon to cut and style your hair before your photo shoot. Don't go cheap on the haircut. Well-cut and well-styled hair will boost your attractiveness and give you greater confidence and presence.

---

10. Guy Kawasaki, *Enchantment* (New York: Penguin Group, 2011), 11.

Eyes. Are you looking directly into the camera? If your eyes look like they are focused away from the lens, you will not look as trustworthy or open.

Eyewear. The rule of thumb has always been to remove your glasses before a photo so there isn't any lighting glare and so as not to put up a barrier between you and the viewer. However, if your glasses are a key part of your visual brand, then by all means wear them. You might consider how well your eyeglass frames are representing the image you want to convey. For a more edgy look, choose a designer who is known for cutting-edge fashion. For a power look, some heavier frames may be appropriate. Pay for thinner lenses since thick, "bottle glass" eyewear is less attractive. If you don't know whether your glasses are enhancing or detracting from your image, have a professional at an optical store discuss the pros and cons of different frames that meet your needs.

Clothing and jewelry. For Twitter photos, I recommend doing a close crop of a photo that shows only your head, so clothes aren't important. However, for a head-and-shoulders shot for LinkedIn, think about what you are trying to convey. If you are trying to move up in your career, dress for the next level. If you are trying to convey a professional but more casual style, wear an open-neck shirt without a tie or jacket. Women should avoid statement necklaces and sparkly jewelry for their photos, as the focus of your photo should be on your face and not your accessories. Choose your clothing colors so that they don't blend into the background.

Facial makeup. A woman's makeup should enhance her beauty, not be a mask. Use a light touch with makeup so it looks natural. A little concealer dabbed under your eyes will eliminate dark circles that can make you look tired. Avoid overdone makeup—too much blush or eye shadow or an overly dark lipstick shade will detract from your professional image.

Both men and women should dust some translucent powder on their faces to reduce shine before a photo session. Your photographer may carry loose powder and a brush for this purpose.

If you want to add more color to your photo, consider being photographed against a colored wall or backdrop. The color should be one that enhances how you look. So if tan or yellow drains the color from your face, don't use these colors in your background. Experiment with color and you will find shades that complement your skin tone and bring out the best in you.

One of my clients was an independent management consultant who wanted to use a photo of himself on a dock with a large fish that he had caught. I understand that people would like to show some of their personality and outside interests, but, in his case, it didn't forward his aim of being taken seriously as a management consultant. The photo did not belong on his home page or in his LinkedIn profile.

In another profile photo example, a young professional woman used a photo of herself in a sleeveless cocktail dress with her hair falling in front of her face. The cocktail dress was not appropriate business attire and her bangs hid half her face. This poor presentation led me to think that she did not have good business judgment. Hopefully your profile photo will encourage introductions and business opportunities, as opposed to discouraging them.

With more people checking you out online before you meet, your profile photo may be the first impression that you give. Make sure that you look your best. And, don't forget to smile.

To Blog or Not to Blog

Blogging is a big commitment, so I don't recommend starting a blog unless:

1. You have something of value to say that can continue for the life of your blog.

2. You have the time to commit to posting regularly—once a week should be the minimum if you want to gain traction with followers. (I am guilty of letting my blog frequency slide when my client work gets too heavy, but I am working on a new editorial schedule that will keep me on track!)

That said, blogging can be an excellent platform for your unique point of view or your thought leadership. It is also more permanent and searchable than posting on, say, Twitter. I started blogging in 2006 and now, even with my somewhat irregular postings, I have a credible compendium of blog articles on branding topics. A number of new clients have told me that my blog helped to sway them to hire me.

> **Blogs can communicate your big ideas, your core values and your personality.**

If you want to evangelize a vision or a way of doing business, writing a blog is an excellent vehicle. Take Tony Hsieh, the CEO of Zappos, which has grown from an online shoe retailer to a customer service organization that "delivers happiness" with a myriad of fashion products. Tony, who is active on Twitter and writes a blog, has been a longtime champion of customer service and culture. His values have evolved into Zappos' present brand promise: Delivering Happiness, also the name of his book. The important thing is that Tony doesn't just talk about these subjects; he and his company live the core values and deliver on what they promise. I have experienced firsthand the authentically friendly customer service reps at Zappos, who make everything easy and bring a smile to your face during the encounter. What Tony did was make his vision and his beliefs public. In doing so, he not only promoted his personal brand, he provided a great lesson on business to the rest of us.

Should You Promote Your Personal Brand or Your Business Brand Online?

Sometimes your personal brand *is* your business brand, as in the case of independent consultants who go by their personal names in business. However, if you have a business brand that is different from your personal name, you still need to have a personal brand.

Your personal brand may not always be tied to your current company. If you are an entrepreneur and you and your company part ways, you need a credible personal brand that can stand on its own as you look to start and fund your next venture. Don't let the VCs or anyone else be the sole shaper of your reputation and image.

A client of mine who is a partner in an international law firm has a plan to be on the boards of large companies in his last few years in law and beyond. One of the ways he is preparing for that transition is using his personal blog to write articles that leverage his law expertise in the broader context of business goals and corporate compliance. He wisely is developing a reputation that is not solely tied to his law firm.

A CEO client who has a start-up company posts on Twitter under his own name as well as having company employees tweet under the company's Twitter account. The CEO's Twitter account shares his passion for open data that goes beyond his company, providing both an intellectual and an emotional connection with his followers.

Online Reputation Management

Managing your online reputation is something everyone should do. It can be as simple as doing a Google search on your name. Are the links and images of you that show up on the first page of search results how you want your brand represented? If not, then you have some work to do.

Unfortunately, items published on the Internet have a long shelf life. However, you can populate your Internet search page results with new and brand-relevant content. Ideas include starting your own website, writing blog posts, commenting on others' blogs, building profiles on popular platforms that rank high in Google searches (for example, LinkedIn, Google+, Facebook), distributing online news releases, and uploading content on YouTube and SlideShare. All of these activities will be found by the search engines and crowd the older items off the first page of results.

You don't have to spend a lot of time managing the online reputation of your personal brand. Follow who mentions you in Twitter, see where you are being tagged in Facebook and sign up for Google Alerts at http://www.google.com/alerts. Recently, Google Alerts made me aware that another site was infringing on my BrandingPays trademark! You certainly want to guard against someone misappropriating your name or image.

Do a Few Things Well

All the social media and social networking services can be daunting.

> **Rather than spread yourself too thin on too many platforms, understand your goals and strategy and choose accordingly.**

If you are new to social media, get on LinkedIn and then choose one more platform on which to focus. Find your voice, build your confidence, provide your unique value and engage with followers.

Chapter 8 Summary

- You must be on social media or lose out on opportunities for jobs, partnerships and the ability to be known by a broader audience for your ideas and expertise.

- Recruiters heavily rely on social networks to find and vet job candidates, so make sure you can be found and are represented well.

- Own your own online real estate with URLs that contain your real name.

- Make your social profile photo one that brands you well.

- Blog only if you have something to say and can sustain it with regular postings.

- Even if you have a company, you need to promote your own personal brand.

Chapter 8 Action List

o   Open social networking accounts, if you haven't already, and make sure that your URL contains your real name.

o   Write a good profile that uses the work that you did in your positioning statement (chapter 2) and messages (chapter 3). Post your profile on the major social networking platforms.

o   Take a high-quality photo of your smiling self and use it consistently as your profile photo on your social networks.

o   Start with LinkedIn and add one or two other social networks, such as Twitter and Facebook.

o   Post content that is 90 percent about business and your field of expertise and 10 percent or less about business-friendly personal stuff.

Conclusion

Reinvent Your Brand for New Opportunities

We've been on an incredible journey together. We've taken you apart and put you back together as a better and reinvented brand. Thank you for being open to new possibilities and new ways to imagine yourself. If nothing else, I hope I have armed you with some 21st-century skills in flexibility, strategic thinking and social networking.

Along the way, we've talked about how a strategic approach to brand positioning and communication is critical to building a credible brand. Icing your cake before you bake it is not advisable. When you jump into tactics and make a lot of noise before you figure out your strategy, you can hinder, rather than help, your brand.

Therefore, we have worked on identifying your strategic recipe for a strong brand. It includes both cake and icing in order to be meaningful and memorable. You have followed the five steps in the BrandingPays™ System to develop your:

Figure C.1

The BrandingPays System works. A great example is a personal branding seminar for up-and-coming female executives that I conducted for a Fortune 100 company. Every participant in the 16-person cohort achieved her desired job or promotion at the company within 12 months of graduating from the BrandingPays series of seminars. Some successfully changed careers, and one graduate went from managing a 40-person staff to managing a 300-person staff in a newly created executive role. These women are living their dreams—largely of their own making. The company benefits from a more diverse talent pool of potential executives and more highly motivated leaders. This seminar series was originally conceived for female executives, but the BrandingPays System is gender neutral and works equally well for men and women.

I am reprising the Personal Branding Journey graphic (Fig. C.2) so you can see how far you have come on your way to reinventing your brand.

Figure C.2

The Branding Journey

How far have you come?

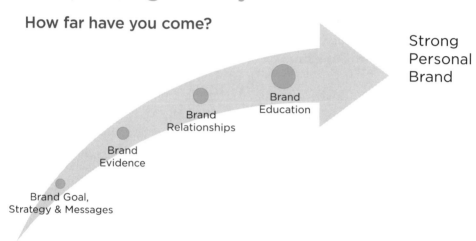

Strong
Personal
Brand

Brand
Education

Brand
Relationships

Brand
Evidence

Brand Goal,
Strategy & Messages

If you have done the action items listed in the book,
you should be well on your way to a better brand.

Personal branding is a skill that will serve you your entire life, whether you follow a straight path or a serendipitous one, as so many of us do. The world is constantly changing, and periodically you will need to rebrand for new opportunities.

I hope that you use *BrandingPays: The Five-Step System to Reinvent Your Personal Brand* as a reference throughout your life and career. Use the positioning statement template to understand how to message to different audiences. Keep your elevator pitch top of mind so you can take advantage of any opportunity—like Jenna, who got a new job by approaching a CEO in a restaurant. Commit to memory your key brand descriptors from the brand strategy platform. They will help to keep you on brand with your cake and icing. Use the ecosystem model to understand and leverage the influencers as your goals or environments change. And, finally, your action plan is a living document that will help to keep you accountable in both brand improvement and brand communication.

I realize that this book may have you feeling that you've just taken a drink from a fire hose. Some of the concepts may feel foreign at first, but with practice the methodology will become easier to master. The clarity that results should give you the confidence to truly brand from the inside out.

You may be starting out and need to create your personal brand, or you may have a brand that you want to reinvent. Whatever your starting point, personal branding will raise your visibility and credibility, and will increase your understanding of your unique value. Whether you are a professional, an entrepreneur or a recent MBA graduate with the goal of a new job, career advancement or business opportunities, personal branding will help you reach your goals.

I want to end this book with some stories about overcoming life and personal branding challenges. I hope you find them as inspiring as I did.

I've enjoyed leading you on this branding journey, and hope that you feel empowered to take charge of your brand.

Four Stories on Overcoming Challenges in Personal Branding and Life

Sherry

Sherry is an African American woman whose parents moved to California after college to avoid the discrimination that they'd experienced in the South. Both of her parents joined large companies and worked hard throughout their careers (one in insurance and the other in retail) to achieve executive roles. Sherry's mother told her young daughter that she needed to be twice as good as her non-black counterparts to get ahead. Bias, she said, continued to exist, as too many people have lingering doubts about promoting blacks as business leaders. Sherry's own parents were often the token person of color in the ranks of upper management.

In 2000, Sherry joined a big biotechnology company as a staff member in Human Resources. She held a variety of positions in staffing and college programs over the next couple of years, and began expanding her responsibilities in the area of diversity. During this time, the company had a critical need for a wider pool of hiring candidates trained in biotech manufacturing. To address this need, Sherry designed and implemented an enterprise program with state workforce boards and local professors to offer a Biotechnology Certificate Program through community colleges. The innovative program, funded by the Department of Labor, was so successful that she testified on Capitol Hill on how the program was achieved.

Sherry completed her master's degree in Organizational Development while working full time and was promoted in 2008 as the director of diversity and inclusion. Despite her apparent career success, she lacked confidence in her new job and felt that management continued to view her as a college programs manager. For the first time, she received a less-than-exemplary review that included critical feedback.

She decided to take action to improve. Sherry enrolled in a six-month leadership skills course and immersed herself in education about diversity, compliance and other subjects key to her performance and diversity expertise.

She took other steps to rebrand herself as a diversity leader. Sherry believed that if she could design and implement an important diversity initiative, her brand would be tied to the program's success. She developed the next generation of workforce strategies and programs to retain and develop women and people of color in science and technology functions. She set goals and milestones, and educated partners and influencers. Two years into the initiative, the company is on track to meet its objectives.

Sherry grew to be a better leader and a better brand by facing her setbacks, learning from her mistakes and taking steps to reach her potential. She did not give in to doubts about her abilities because of her gender, race or background.

> **When the little voice of doubt started nagging at her and eroding her confidence, she acknowledged it but did not let it grow.**

She was the inspirational speaker at a recent corporate event attended by more than 200 employees and key executive leaders, including the company CEO. Today, Sherry is seen as *the* diversity leader at her company and a shining example of the company's own diversity policies.

Ahmad

Ahmad, a gay Malaysian immigrant, is a business banking executive in a large San Francisco bank. His personal branding journey is a testament to his drive and determination to succeed despite the odds.

Ahmad was born in a poor Muslim village in Malaysia to an illiterate mother who worked in a factory on a rubber plantation and a father who worked in a sawmill. Ahmad and his five siblings lived in a house with no running water or electricity. It was a struggle to keep food on the table and adequate clothing on the children.

Education was Ahmad's ticket out of poverty. His siblings, who lacked his ambition, are still in Malaysia working in farming and factory jobs. The only one in his family to speak a foreign language, Ahmad learned English so he could get a job as a waiter at a Malaysian resort. He spent seven years in hospitality in Malaysia and Vietnam before working with an international agent to find an assistant finance job in a fancy California hotel and resort on the Pacific Ocean.

Tired of resorts nestled in trees, Ahmad became a front office manager for a San Francisco hotel. Soon after the 9/11 terrorist attack that destroyed the World Trade Center, he lost his job because travel and tourism dried up in the aftermath. He started working morning and night shifts in two different jobs to survive financially. He began thinking of his future. Ahmad decided to leave the uncertainty of hospitality and forge a new career in banking based on his sales and financial analysis skills.

A contact within a large San Francisco bank told him about some sales openings in personal banking and provided him with a reference. Each time Ahmad went for interviews, he met with a Caucasian executive who looked at him skeptically. What they saw was someone from hospitality who had no banking experience, who looked and sounded foreign with a strange name and accent, and who had an effeminate voice and body language. According to Ahmad, the bank organization was open to diversity but the actual employees held their own personal biases. He was rejected for three separate jobs. Finally, in his fourth and final try, he found a female executive willing to give him a chance. He got a job as a personal banking officer.

Ahmad knew he had to prove himself and worked doubly hard to exceed the expectations of those who harbored doubts about his ability.

He took every personal development and banking course that his bank offered. His friendly personality, sense of humor and excellent customer service skills from his hospitality experience won over new banking customers. While working full time, Ahmad went to college at night and finished his degree in business administration with honors. He will also soon be taking his test to become a U.S. citizen. The bank recognized his industry and track record, and he repeatedly won awards as a top producer. After three promotions, he is currently an assistant vice president in business banking.

Ahmad has faced discrimination in Malaysia for coming from a poor family and for being gay in a strict Muslim community. He has faced bias as a short Asian man, an immigrant with an accent, a Muslim in America, a gay outsider, and a business banker who lacks an MBA degree. His advice?

Change what you can, but don't dwell on things you can't change or control.

He believes that people have control over 90 percent of their personal brand, and this is where you should put your focus. Ahmad has learned to take risks and to stretch himself in his career. He already has his sights on his next career move in banking that will leverage his trilingual capabilities and his international experience. He is building his résumé and shifting his brand to position himself for the next chapter in his amazing story.

Modesta

Modesta was the fifth out of six daughters born to Mexican-Americans who started their life as farm workers in East Texas. Her mother rose early each morning to make tortillas and pack lunches for the family workers. She then went to pick cotton in the hot sun—even when she was pregnant.

Modesta's parents had no formal education. They wished for a better life for their children.

The ultimate dream was a high school diploma for each of their daughters. College, a standard milestone for middle-class children, was not even a consideration.

When Modesta was old enough for high school, she moved in with her sister and brother-in-law and took care of their children. Modesta attended a small Catholic high school where many of the students' parents were the town's business owners and power brokers. The expectations for the students of color—less than a dozen at her school—were not high. In fact, on the day that college representatives visited their high school, neither Modesta nor the other students of color were invited to attend.

When she graduated from high school, Modesta moved in with relatives in California. As a Latina and the daughter of manual laborers, she was conditioned to have low expectations for her life. However, she enrolled in the local community college and found a mentor, a Mexican-American educator who changed her life. He saw in her promise that no one else had seen. He encouraged her to run for president of La Raza, the Chicano student group he advised. She wanted to be of service, so she worked hard to get over her painful shyness and won the election. Modesta gained new confidence and has never looked back.

With the help of multiple college mentors who convinced her that she was smart and capable, and as a Ford Foundation Scholar, she transferred to the University of Santa Clara and studied in Europe. She later attended Harvard University for her master's in Education. Throughout her life, Modesta had few role models and, at times, felt the sting of bias as a Latina in a white man's world. In spite of her humble background and cultural challenges, she succeeded.

Princeton University hired her as an admissions officer, starting her on a career path in counseling and college admissions. In her long career, Harvard and national organizations have recognized Modesta for service leadership in education. She has always had a passion for service, and recently retired from her job as a community college academic and career counselor. Helping community college students—especially multicultural students—to dream big was her way of giving back and honoring all of the mentors who had believed in her when she was young.

Modesta has now started her second act. She founded her own college admissions counseling business and is learning to rebrand as an entrepreneur. We worked together on her brand positioning as an independent counselor and coach for college admissions. In addition to her Ivy League experience, she has consulted in Asia on college planning and admissions. Few college admissions consultants can match her cake: a Latina with strong educational counseling credentials, Ivy League education and admissions experience, and placement success with diverse students, including students of color and international students. Her icing is her empathy and her passion for serving the underrepresented in particular, and the global student demographic in general. Modesta has proven that professional ambitions and cultural values do not have to be mutually exclusive.

> **Modesta has a tip for those who want a higher-visibility brand: engage in *meaningful volunteerism.***

She volunteers tirelessly as a counselor, speaker and organizer for myriad groups that serve underrepresented communities. She spent years organizing programs with her local alumni group, the Harvard Club, and was rewarded with the top leadership position. It was no small feat given that she was the first person of color and only the third woman to be elected president of this former bastion of white men. Thanks to Modesta's leadership, her area's Harvard Club now has a diverse board. This visibility and credibility as a counselor and speaker has enabled her to serve youth, with the unexpected benefit of enhanced job choices and key business connections.

> **Modesta went from a shy girl who thought menial labor was her destiny to being a force for change in the Ivy League.**

Her story is an inspiration for anyone who must overcome challenges to achieve a desired brand.

Doreen

Doreen Woo Ho is a former *Time* magazine foreign correspondent and longtime banking executive with Citicorp, Wells Fargo and United Commercial Bank, where she served as president and CEO. While retired from any operating roles in banking, she is currently an independent director on the board of directors of US Bancorp. She is also the president of the San Francisco Port Commission that oversees the 7.5 miles of San Francisco waterfront, including many real estate development projects. She is a graduate of Smith College and Columbia University.

What follows is her story and advice for Asian Americans on success in personal branding.

Doreen's Story

Doreen was born in Australia to a Taiwanese diplomat and his wife. After living in Sydney for eight years and attending an English-speaking school, she moved to Taiwan, where her father had been reposted. Going from a highly developed Western economy and standard of living to the relative undeveloped environment of Taiwan was shocking. Instead of cars, there were people-powered pedicabs. Instead of indoor toilets, there were outhouses with no plumbing. Because her parents had spoken English at home in Australia, Doreen and her older brother had to learn Chinese. Despite the difficulties she faced, Doreen remembers her time in Taiwan as a happy one.

After three years in Taiwan, her father moved the family to his new diplomatic post in Tokyo, where they lived for a year. Then, her father was posted to West Africa as the ambassador to Cameroon and Togo. Thinking that the West Africa post was temporary and concerned about the lack of good schools, the parents sent Doreen and her brother to boarding schools in the United States. Little did Doreen know that she would not see her parents again for five years! Taiwanese diplomatic salaries were low, and the family could not afford the costly travel between West Africa and the United States.

Thus, Doreen became independent at the age of 13. Luckily, her family circumstances made her readily adaptable to change. She always saw moving as a new adventure. A fortune-teller once told her mother that Doreen's personality was "like a rolling stone with no moss."

The stereotype of Asians, Doreen says, is that they avoid risks. In her own career, she has taken a number of them. Instead of continuing in a safe job with a bank, she accepted a job at the age of 22 as a Vietnam War correspondent in Cambodia, resulting from a chance meeting with the Time magazine bureau chief at a cocktail party. "I guess I made a good impression," she says of the subsequent job offer she received.

She again took a risk with her then-husband to relocate back to the United States instead of Asia just before the fall of Cambodia and Saigon. She was accepted into Citibank's management training program and chose to enroll in the program in San Francisco. A cross-country move might not seem daunting if you have been a "rolling stone" for most of your life.

Doreen's adaptability and ability to make big decisions were on display even when she was an undergraduate at Smith College, an elite all-women's college in Massachusetts. A Life magazine article on human reproduction had inspired her to major in biochemistry, but by her junior year, she was tired of the time spent alone in a lab. She realized that she was a people person and switched to being a history major.

Ivy League schools were all-male institutions when she went to Smith, and she recalls that most of the Smith students seemed more interested in getting married than in pursuing a career. However, Doreen had greater ambitions. She has always had the need to move forward, use her brain and be challenged in ways that being a stay-at-home mom could never satisfy. Yet she is the proud mother of three children, all college graduates and pursuing their own careers. She readily admits that a helpful husband and a housekeeper assisted her in managing a demanding executive career and family life.

There is a time and a place for everything. Doreen's career was not a straight trajectory to the top. "Careers zigzag. I consciously chose some lateral staff positions to reduce the amount of travel and my workload," she says of juggling career and young children. "I tell people it's okay to do that."

Asian Americans Can Overcome Personal Branding Challenges

Personal branding can be a challenge for anyone, but it can be especially hard for Asians.

> Changing the racial stereotype of Asians as meek geeks requires that they be more visible, stronger leaders and better at self-marketing.

The latter is hard for many Asians who have been taught that humility, quiet deference and respect for authority are key values.

American business icons often have big personalities, big egos and aren't afraid of confrontation or risk. Think of Steve Jobs, Larry Ellison, and on a gentler vector, Oprah Winfrey. But when I think about iconic Asian business leaders, my mind draws a blank. Why aren't Asian business leaders household names? In a nutshell, they lack powerful personal brands.

I asked Doreen how Asians can overcome personal branding challenges.

She advises Asians to get outside the stereotype of the passive worker who is good at numbers but not so good with people or management skills. They should be proud of their culture and heritage, she says, but not make being Asian the prime identifier of their brand.

Her personal branding advice is important for anyone, regardless of race, gender or cultural heritage:

- You are a professional, who just happens to be Asian or a woman or...

- Welcome change and new challenges.

- Hone your written and verbal skills. You've got to be able to sell your ideas.

> **Learn to transition from being an excellent doer to an excellent leader who achieves through inspiring and motivating others.**

- It takes more than IQ (intelligence quotient) and EQ (emotional quotient) to be a strong leader—add the third ingredient, MQ (meaningful quotient). Help people understand how they fit into the vision and the value they bring as an individual.

- Don't just focus on getting your job done; spend time on relating to people and cultivating relationships—especially with career influencers.

- When you climb the executive ladder, understand that the intangible attributes become more important (how strategically you think, how you solve problems, how you lead).

- Develop an ease of socializing inside and outside the office. Breaking into the inner circle of executives is more about personal chemistry and homogeneous backgrounds. Executives feel more comfortable around people who share common experiences.

Finally, Doreen says, don't let racial or other stereotypes get you down—focus on doing your job. Doreen was almost kept from traveling to South America to handle some client problems because she was thought of as the "China doll" by her customer, a VP of Finance at a sizable private company. He believed that she couldn't hold her own in the macho environment of Brazil and Venezuela. She took the trip with another male executive and fixed the problem. Ironically, the local bank officers at the Citibank branches that she dealt with in South America were all women! So much for stereotypes.

Doreen hopes that others characterize her leadership brand as:

- An inspiring and visionary leader who sets stretch goals
- A tough manager who takes on challenges and delivers results
- A caring leader who mentors others

She derives great satisfaction from having mentored a number of professionals, including those reaching the C-suite in large companies. She advises young professionals that mentors choose their mentees based on a personal or professional connection. Mentees don't get to choose their mentors unless there is a mutual benefit, she says.

Final Words of Advice

"You have to develop a brand because everyone needs to develop a brand to be successful," Doreen advises. "You have to have all the qualities. You have to look the part, look professional and be pleasant. You have to have the communication skills." She says that Asian parents stress math skills with their children and spend less time on encouraging good written and verbal skills.

"You may have the best content in the world . . . but you have to figure out how to sell and communicate it in a way that people will buy and appreciate it." The same can be said of personal brands.

Further Reading

Crossing the Chasm
by Geoffrey A. Moore

If you are an entrepreneur, this book is a must-read classic. It applies
the Technology Adoption Cycle to technology markets, and identifies the
"chasm" between the risk-taking early adopters and the more conservative
mainstream customers. *BrandingPays*™ adopts Moore's positioning
statement template for personal branding.

Relationship Marketing (first published as *The Regis Touch*)
by Regis McKenna

Relationship Marketing, an iconic marketing book, explains how
relationships are key to winning customers, and how traditional advertising
and PR are dead. This book lays the foundation for many of the positioning
and influencer concepts found in *BrandingPays*.

Enchantment
by Guy Kawasaki

Guy Kawasaki is a best-selling author, the former Apple chief evangelist
and the founder of Garage Ventures and Alltop. *Enchantment* is his
all-in-one guidebook for branding yourself, a product or a company. Like me,
he believes in branding from the inside out, and starts with the need to be
likable and how to influence people. This book includes many of the themes
in Dale Carnegie's landmark book, *How to Win Friends and Influence
People,* but is updated for the age of social media.

Sway: The Irresistible Pull of Irrational Behavior
by Ori Brafman and Rom Brafman

I've included this book because it is eye-opening to learn how irrational
we are when it comes to what sways our perceptions and behaviors. The
Brafman brothers make an excellent case for the importance of what I call
"icing" in *BrandingPays*.

Impressive First Impressions
by Vu H. Pham and Lisa Miyake

This is a practical and comprehensive guide to actions we can take to guide the impression we make on others—something fundamental to personal branding.

Me 2.0
by Dan Schawbel

This book is geared mainly toward Millennials who want to brand themselves for the job market. Dan Schawbel provides basic information on personal branding concepts and practical advice on how to use social media to find a job. He created a popular blog at www.personalbrandingblog.com that has useful articles by a host of contributors.

The New Rules of Marketing and PR
by David Meerman Scott

Although David Meerman Scott wrote this book for marketers in companies, his excellent advice on social media works for building personal brands as well.

Own Your Niche
by Stephanie Chandler

Stephanie Chandler targets people in service-based businesses who want to claim their authority and leverage the Internet to sell their services. Her practical tips and entrepreneur interviews are relevant to individuals who want to brand themselves. This easy-to-read book is geared toward beginners.

Resonate and Slide:ology: The Art and Science
of Creating Great Presentations
by Nancy Duarte

Nancy Duarte, who gained fame for helping Al Gore with his Inconvenient
Truth slide show, lays out the philosophy and elements that it takes to
develop and deliver a great presentation. Since presentations are so
important to positioning yourself and your ideas in your career, Duarte's
books can help you tell a compelling story with words and images.

The Brand Gap
by Marty Neumeier

Marty Neumeier's small book is a classic among branding professionals.
It cuts to the chase of what brand is all about: "The foundation of brand is
trust." Read the final section on "Take-Home Lessons" for a pithy summary
of his key points—a lot of truth packed into a few pages. He talks about
branding companies, services and products, but he could well be talking
about people. You are the product!

Index

Acknowledgments

I am grateful to so many people who have helped me throughout my career and, more recently, with their support for this book.

As many writers come to realize, writing can be a lonely profession. There were dark days when I wondered if this book would ever see the light of day. Without the love and support of my husband, Jon Ferraiolo, I don't think the book would have ever happened. My three adult daughters, Nikki, Natalie and Allie, were a constant source of inspiration with their own branding journeys and the authentic way they lead their lives. My sister, Valerie, inspired me with her career transformation, and my brother, Steve, gave me his support and valuable feedback.

I am deeply indebted to Karla Olson, my book shepherd, who was instrumental in guiding my writing and setting up the book production and distribution. While working with me, Karla actually used the BrandingPays™ System to get her dream job as Director of Patagonia Books. She introduced me to Marika Flatt and her excellent team at PR by the Book, who have handled my book publicity. Helen Chang helped me craft the original outline for my book, which was the boost I needed to write the book.

I would like to express gratitude to my initial BrandingPays™ Certified Consultants—Meta Mehling, Steven Kang, Carol Anglin, Claire Chang and Ellen Taverner—for their constant support, book feedback and

and Ellen Taverner—for their constant support, book feedback and the sharing of their client success stories. I am indebted to other early readers as well: Seymour Duncker, Cristina Nogueira, Leonard Lodish, Rene Siegal, Larry Chang and Satya Krishnaswamy.

Thank you . . .

To those who have shared their stories with me: Doreen Woo Ho, Modesta Garcia, Randy Paynter, Michael Dreyfus, Lisa Hammann, Caryn McDowell, Kate Kendall, Murat Wahab, Monica Poindexter, Roxanne de la Riva, Siddika Demir, Gisela Paulsen, Greg Chung, Hillary Freeman and many others unnamed.

To my friends, colleagues and clients at Humpal, Leftwich & Sinn, Tycer-Fultz-Bellack and Regis McKenna Inc., who helped me to develop as a leader and consultant, and showed me what fun business can be. Dan Bellack, thank you for being a great boss and mentor. Don Kobrin, thanks for the decades of lunches that have challenged and inspired me. Susan Faraone, thanks for your friendship and support. Paul Sinn and Mark Galarneau, thanks for teaching me about good design.

To Regis McKenna for being a mentor and a model for visionary thinking.

To Geoffrey Moore for paving the way with *Crossing the Chasm,* and making me believe I could make a difference with my book.

To Leslie Guidice and Stacy Guidice at Energy Energy Design for their great visual designs for BrandingPays and more than a decade of collaboration on client brands.

To Debra Kopelman, Tanja Miller and Don Kraft for believing in my personal branding methodology and setting up the successful seminar series at Genentech.

To others who have helped along the way: Susan Lucas-Conwell,
Raj Setty, Tamiko Wong, Adam Helweh, Shiva Kumar, Carol Pecora,
Will Price, Steve Morozumi, Pinky Cheung, Jack Koch and my
wonderful clients, who teach me new things every day.

To my dear friends who renew my spirit with their love and humor:
Laurie Duncan, Amy Mishima Petersen, Maureen McNulty,
Hillary Freeman, Nancy Lytle, Pam Kline Smith, Laura Elmore,
and my longtime friends at Thursday Morning Dialogue.

About the Author

Karen Kang is a recognized brand strategist and the founder and CEO of BrandingPays LLC, a corporate and personal branding company (www.brandingpays.com). She has trained thousands of professionals on the unique BrandingPays™ System for personal branding.

Karen was a partner with Regis McKenna Inc., the legendary marketing firm that created and launched the Apple brand. She has consulted to more than 150 organizations in the United States, Europe and Asia, from Fortune 100 companies to nonprofits and start-ups. Her broad experience has included such diverse clients as Ariba, AT&T, Genentech, HP, iCharts, Lavante, Synopsys, Maxtor, NCR, Park Systems, SigmaQuest (Camstar), UC Davis Health System, Webroot and VoyagePrive.

Karen's marketing and communications background gives her a 360-degree view of branding. A former newspaper journalist on both the East and West Coasts, she has held executive positions in marketing consulting, advertising and public relations firms. Karen is a frequent speaker at leading business schools and professional organizations.

She has served on the board of Friends of the Palo Alto Library and the advisory board of the Women's Technology Cluster (Astia). She has also donated her time to such worthy nonprofit organizations as Girls for a Change, CORO, Asian Business League of San Francisco and Ascend. Karen is a member of Phi Beta Kappa and graduated with a B.A. degree in English from Mills College. She earned her M.S. degree in Journalism from Boston University.

Follow her on Twitter @karenkang and connect on Facebook at www.facebook.com/BrandingPays.

Accelerate Your Personal Branding Journey

Karen Kang's BrandingPays™ offers a number of ways to help you on your personal branding journey.

Go to the BrandingPays™ site at www.BrandingPays.com to:

* Sign up for the free newsletter with branding tips and resources
* Follow the BrandingPays Blog
* Connect with Karen on Twitter, Facebook, LinkedIn and Google+
* Learn about upcoming seminars and coaching packages

Engage in the Twitter conversation by using the hashtag #BrandingPays in your tweets. Karen will reply to the best questions and retweet the best ideas.

Like our Facebook page at www.facebook.com/BrandingPays, post comments and check out our events.

Personal Branding Webinars and Seminars

Join Karen in webinars and seminars that provide an engaging way to learn the BrandingPays System and apply it to your career. Stories and examples help to illustrate concepts. Interactive questions and answers provide a customized learning opportunity. In-person seminars include group breakout exercises for collaboration and networking.

BrandingPays Web Tools

All BrandingPays personal branding clients and paid webinar/seminar participants get access to our web tools that complement the BrandingPays System. The tools work with all major web browsers, and provide interactive templates, tips and an online repository for your branding work.

Book Karen Kang
for Your Next Event!

Author and branding expert Karen Kang is a sought-after speaker for conferences, company events and graduate schools of business. She has addressed a wide range of audiences from top executives to graduate business students, law firms to health care organizations, diversity councils to women's leadership groups.

An inspiring and engaging speaker, she is available for featured speaking engagements and seminars. A partial list of her featured speaking events and seminar engagements:

London Business School
Stanford University
Barnard College
Wharton School, University of Pennsylvania
Haas School, University of California at Berkeley
Boston University School of Management
UC San Diego Medical School
National Retail Federation
Women at Intel Annual Conference
Asian Pacific Bar Association of Silicon Valley
Ascend West Coast Conference
Genentech
SV Forum
Forum for Women Entrepreneurs (Watermark)
Social Media Club of Seattle
Korean-American Chamber of Commerce
CORO
Intrax
City of Chula Vista
Vistage International
McKesson PAVE Asian Heritage Month
Asian Professional Women in Technology
Asian Women in Business
Women's Technology Cluster (Astia)
Toastmasters (District 4 Fall Conference)
Leadership Palo Alto (Palo Alto Chamber of Commerce)
National Association of Asian MBAs

Visit www.BrandingPays.com/event-speaking for more information.